(

BEFORE THE SILENCE

Fifty years in the history
of Alderville First Nation

BEFORE THE SILENCE

Fifty years in the history
of Alderville First Nation

1825-1875

by Ruth Clarke

ISBN— 0-9685572-0-1

Cover paintings and illustrations:
front cover painting, "Portage to Rice Lake"
back cover painting, "Woodland Inspection"
frontispiece painting, "Tomorrow"
text illustrations:
page 40, "Woodland Inspection"
page 60, "Portage to Rice Lake"
page 66, "Love Among Thorns"
all © Rick Beaver, 1999 Sweetgrass Studios,
Alderville First Nation, Ontario, Canada.

photograph of the author: Roy Diment

Design, typesetting and production: Roy Diment
Vivencia Resources Group, Victoria, BC. Canada

The author gratefully acknowledges the support of the Canada Council, Ontario Arts Council, and Ontario Heritage Foundation for research and writing grants.

Printed 1999 in Canada by:
Fleming Printing Ltd. Victoria, BC

Contents

Acknowledgements

Words can effectively express many feelings, but often sound cliché when it comes to declaring gratitude. I'll try anyway. Firstly, I am grateful for ever being introduced to the people of Alderville—especially John Loukes, who invited me to write this history. Thanks to Nora Bothwell, who was Chief at the time, to her council and staff for their enthusiasm and support. To David Mowat, whom Chief and Council hired to help me research, and for his ensuing friendship and support. To Melody Crowe, for providing local dialect for the Ojibway used in the book, and for her friendship and enthusiasm for the project. Thanks to Reverend Murray Whetung of Curve Lake and minister at the Alderville United Church, for consulting with Melody on some Ojibway phrases. Thanks to Merilyn Simonds for her initial interest and continuing support for the way I was approaching the material, for her eyes and her expertise, and for writing the foreword for this book. Thanks to the Canada Council, the Ontario Heritage Foundation and the Ontario Arts Council, for the grants I was awarded to research and write, and to Pat Parnall at Fleming College for filling in the fiscal gaps by hiring me part-time. To the Reverends William Lamb, Arthur Kewley, Elgie Joblin and Gordon Ficko for providing background when I began my research. To Audrey Gognavec, Marg Miner and Shirley Rochon from Parry Island, descendants of Allan Salt. To Susan Crean, Mark Finnan and Drs. Ian Johnson and John Milloy for their support for the project.

The emotional support of friends has been a strength, their patience a comfort. I am grateful to the grandmothers, mothers, daughters and granddaughters of the Full Moon Circle, who made me welcome. Special thanks to George Charles and Gail McLaren for keeping the bond—for keeping me connected—when I went to away to write the first draft. Gracias a mis amigos en Costa Rica por la amistad durante el año que estube allá. Gracias a Gerardo Bolaños, la familia Bolaños, a Jorge Oviedo, hermano y amigo para siempre. Thanks to Rick Beaver for his patient, caring ways, his sensitivity, understanding and vision.

I am most grateful to Chief Wesley Marsden and his council who revived this project almost ten years later.

This book is dedicated to the
people of Alderville First Nation.

Foreword

History, since the beginning of written record, has been a blend of chronicle and myth, event and narrative: the human imagination attempting to make sense of the chaos of the past. George Woodcock, in "The Monk and his Message: Undermining the Myth of History", describes Herodotus, the first historian, as a man who "sought those plausible fictions, constructed largely out of facts, which are necessary for the human mind to penetrate the sheer disorder of actual process and existence."

The dual demands of writing history, always a challenge, became a burden in the scientific age. History simply refused to become an exact science. Digging up and assessing facts does have something of the scientific about it, but there is more art than science to the discipline. As anyone who has dabbled in the field soon discovers, facts alone have little relevance.

To be comprehensible, they must be arranged. Even then, the patterns continually shift, depending on who is doing the selecting and the organizing, and what societal forces are acting upon the process. The gaps between what is known must be bridged with what is likely, what might have been, and here the historian leaves the realm of science, leaning heavily on the arm of the whimsical Clio, muse of both poetry and history.

Nowhere are the shifting patterns of history more apparent than in the reconstruction of early contact between Europeans and Native peoples on this continent. For centuries the story has been written by the conquerors, played out against a landscape called "the New World" despite the fact that it was inhabited 20,000 years before Columbus and Cabot set sail from Europe, heading into the sunset. Places that had been known for generations were suddenly renamed for landscapes thousands of miles away, a process that Peter McFarlane and Wayne Haimila in their book "Ancient Land, Ancient Sky" call "death by cartography." But now history is being rewritten again, and yet again, the story retold from fresh perspectives, through Native eyes. The old languages, the old place names are returning, emerging, as Wayne Grady writes in Equinox magazine (June/July 1999) "like long-dormant tendrils through the leaf litter of the centuries."

No one can know for certain what life was like "before the silence" that fell over the natives of southeastern Ontario. But history is not about certainty. Deeply embedded in the word is the notion of "story" and this is what Ruth Clarke delivers: a tale of Methodist conversion of the remains of an Ojibway band in the first years of the last century, a recreation-and a revelation - of that moment when settlement irrevocably triumphed over the nomadic native life.

"Before the Silence" is part of a significant and growing movement to reclaim native history. As such, it adds another facet to our understanding of the evolution of the nation we call Canada. It boldly recreates, through document and informed imagination, the particulars of a past that can never be completely known. This in no way detracts from its veracity. As Woodcock concludes, "So long as history is oriented towards the past, it remains tentative and to that extent, true."

Merilyn Simonds
Kingston, Ontario

Preface

The people of Alderville First Nation are descendants of Mississauga Ojibway: Mississauga signifying people who live in a country where there are many mouths of rivers.[1] Ojibway is the name given to the people whose *makizinan*[2] have puckered seams. They are a tribe of the Algonkin Nation. At the beginning of the 19th century, there were some fifteen families—among them Beavers, Crows, Sundays and Simpsons [or what their names were before they became anglicized]. They were survivors from bands of the Kingston and Ganonoque *Mississauga Ojibway*—trying unsuccessfully to live by hunting and fishing in an area that since 1783 had been surveyed by the ruling government of Britain for settlement.

By the 1820s, the population of Kingston Township exceeded 100,000 inhabitants and the only unoccupied land from Kingston to the Bay of Quinte were islands and geographical backwaters. Indians were being driven off land then known as Upper Canada, land they'd known intimately for more than one hundred years.

Methodism—or the Methodist Movement—was an evangelical school of Protestant Christianity. It appealed to the common man, to the helpless and to the hopeless, and to the converted—who gave them money. The Indians called the Methodists the Black Coat men, and attended their "love feasts" or camp meetings—days of impassioned religious exhortations and conversions in meadows filled with settlers, whom the Indians called the Hats because they all wore coverings on their heads.

Reverend William Case was one of the leaders in the Movement; before there were churches he was a circuit—or itinerant—minister who earned the name Father of Indian Missions.

The government supported Case's idea to gather all of the wandering "savage heathens" together, away from the bad influences of white settlers. Case chose Grape Island: eleven-acres of land three miles out in the Bay of Quinte in Lake Ontario, to build his dream. On Grape Island, the Mississaugas were groomed to be Methodists, forced to abandon their language and culture, their old ways silenced with the promise that if their children learned English they could become lawyers, doctors, and teachers, like white people. With the promise of a more prosperous way of life, the *Mississaugas* shed their traditions and customs. Farming would replace hunting and fishing as a means of subsistence.

Sixteen Mississauga Ojibway men from Grape Island became missionaries to northern tribes and later to western Canada. Among them was *Shawundais*, or John Sunday, who'd fought in the War of 1812 and had been part of the post-war exodus from his birthplace in New York State, to Upper Canada. He'd already seen the effects of encroaching settlement, the subjugation his people were suffering, and wanted them to feel empowered like him, with his new-found saviour.

With the first conversion of the *Mississaugas* in the Bay of Quinte area on May 31, 1826, a Society of Methodist Indians was organized on Grape Island: a Methodist landmark to be remembered as the Nursery of Indian Missions. The converted Indians cleared the land and although they first lived in *wiigwaaman*, they eventually constructed log houses, a church, a hospital and a schoolhouse. The women canoed or snowshoed to a nearby island to feed and milk cattle; crops were tended on another.

Grape Island's popularity among the displaced Indian population of the area was deemed successful by the Methodist Movement but the stress for the great numbers of people – at one point, more than two hundred— living in such cramped quarters proved unhealthy and often fatal. The influx of disease dangerously decreased their numbers, and by 1831, the government was advising John Sunday to choose land where his people wanted to live so it could be surveyed into lots for them.

While I could find no reference to the reasoning behind John Sunday's decision to relocate to the Rice Lake area, it seems most logical and appropriate, since historically, the lake had been a healing place where Indians brought their ailing elders. They had gone to fish there in summer, to gather wild rice at summer's end and to hunt waterfowl that fed on the rice beds in the fall. Soil samples taken on East Sugar Island by Alderville students during an archaeological dig for the Royal Ontario Museum in 1973 revealed that their ancestors had been growing wild rice there for more than 9,000 years.[3] It is still in living memory when the stalks grew shoulder high and each family hauled 300-400 pounds in the harvest.

Methodist reports and statistics of what *Ojibway* women from Grape Island were producing, or how they were progressing, attest to their hard work. However, personal accounts are absent from any research I was able to find. Thankfully, authors like Basil Johnson, Ruth Landes et al, and the contributors of the Curve Lake history books have documented Ojibway traditions and I could have an inkling of the rich Ojibway culture prior to contact with the Methodists.

In 1989, I was invited by Chief and Council to write the history of Alderville First Nation, from its earlier times at Grape Island to present day, a span of 163 years. As a reporter for an area newspaper, I was aware of their more recent history, but little else about these people. So, in taking on the project, I cast a wide net, gathering archival materials, but also collecting more recent photographs, and conducting interviews with a number of people on the reserve.

What I realized was that the material was too vast for one book. And that the fifty years from 1825-1875 told a story: it had a beginning, a middle and an end to a significant period that has shaped and affected how Alderville has since evolved. More recent history of Alderville will be published in a second volume of photographs, interviews and anecdotes.

Throughout the book, the *Mississaugas* and other tribes are referred to as "Indians" or "Native people"; the former was used during that period in history, and continues to be used today by many of the people of Alderville First Nation. To "talk Indian" is how they refer to speaking *Ojibway*. Other times they refer to themselves as Native people, so I have used both terms wherever it seemed appropriate.

Sources for this book used several spellings for the same word, and are the result of different dialects of Ojibway—a name that is also spelled Ojebway, Ojibwa and Ojibwe. The Ojibway language dialect for this southern Ontario region uses a double vowel writing system. There are three short vowels: i as in hill or pin; a is pronounced uh as in run or fun, and o as in look or tomorrow. There are also four long vowels: ii as in see and me; aa as in saw or taught; oo as in phone or moon. The single e is also a long vowel and is pronounced like the a in that or cat. Chi miigwech to Melody Crowe for providing this explanation and local interpretation.

Before the Silence is a period in history seen through the eyes of *Ishpiniibin*, a young *Mississauga* woman, who will soon be named Sarah by the Methodists. Orphaned before her teenage years, she lives with her aunt and uncle *Shawundais*, who is soon to be christened John Sunday. He will become a Native missionary who began his Christian life on Grape Island.

Dates, facts and statistics surrounding the events mentioned in the book are factual and referenced. However, nothing exists from this period that tells the story from a woman's point of view. Sarah's character emerged from the research and helps to illustrate the acute contrast her people experienced as they abandoned their old ways, and adopted a new way of life.

Before The Silence

A sliver of *Waabab'gaa Giizis*—the Leaves Turning Colour Moon—rises above the bay, her delicate but penetrating light slashing the water like shards of a broken mirror. At the shoreline, *Ishpiniibin*, a girl of some twelve summers, holds a small baby in her arms. She watches one of the men drop leaves of tobacco on the still water. By a campfire down the shore, a lone drummer sings while the men ask *Chi Mnidoo* to be generous to them. Soon, when ice covers the lake, they will leave their summer camp and travel north to hunt. Some of them pray while a limp black dog is rolled over the gunnels of the canoe into the water, a sacrificial gift for the Creator.

"*Mnidoo ahaw.*" The girl breathes the response with them; the words curl from her mouth like puffs of smoke rising in the cool air. The baby wriggles beneath the blanket that covers them both. Though there is frost in the air, sweat beads the tiny girl's face. Her breath is laboured. She has drifted in and out of a fever since before *Miin giizis;*[4] her lungs scream with a pain no poultice can draw, no tea can soothe.

The baby is the child of *Ishpiniibin's* aunt who now mourns the two boys she's lost to the Land of Souls, victims of one of the many diseases the Hats brought here with them. In the past winter, *Ishpiniibin's* mother and father died too—from scarlet fever or measles, or maybe cholera—all deadly to her people who have neither the strength nor the medicines needed to fight them. When her mother and father were alive, the two families shared one *wiigwaam*. Now she lives with the baby's parents—*Shawundais* and his wife, and grandmother. The lodge feels vast, empty without her mother and father.

Ishpiniibin had watched as her aunt blackened her face with coal, tears streaming, the day she buried her boys. Beyond the charcoal, the burden of the woman's sorrow drew rigid lines in her face. The woman covers her body in only the dirtiest of rags now, and never bathes. She fasted for many days after her sons' deaths, and though she eats a little more now, each day she still takes some of her food to their little graves.[5]

Only the baby is left. They pray that the Great Spirit will ease her suffering, that He will be gentle with her, but there is little hope that her fragile life will last until the *Bnaakwii Giizis*—the Falling Leaves Moon. *Ishpiniibin* cradles the infant.

Outlines of the men smoulder above the rippling water; their pine torches spotlights for surfacing fish the men jab with their spears.[6]

Ishpiniibin's name celebrates the rewards of harvest time. Born past the middle of *Niibin*—the Abundant Season—she has seen the coming and going of bountiful—and—of scarce seasons. Her name was the gift of a medicine woman at her *Wawiindaassowin*—her Naming Ceremony, the most important ceremony of life—when she was three years old.[7]

When she was born, her mother and father had called her Jumping Fawn: the animal that appeared before her father at the time of her birth. First swaddled in a bundleboard where she squirmed and boxed her tight little fists at the air around her, the name had little relation to her feisty nature. But after she took her first steps, her energetic little legs kept moving, and the name fit.

During Jumping Fawn's third summer, her mother and father asked her mother's aged aunt, a medicine woman, to give the child a name. To find the name, Medicine Woman sought guidance through visions and messages that came to her during meditation and dreaming. The name came to the old woman in a dream some time later, and the day after the dream, Medicine Woman announced that the ceremony would be held in four days.

To prepare for the day, Medicine Woman cleaned her lodge, and placed fresh cedar boughs on the floor. The girl's parents gave the namer gifts; Medicine Woman in turn, bestowed blessings from the *Mnidoos*: gifts she'd been given during her puberty fast, long ago. These gifts would be useful to the girl until it was time for her own puberty fast.[8]

Medicine Woman then gathered the flowers of late summer, leaves, roots and seeds of healing plants, wrapped them in a doeskin bundle, and during the ceremonial feast, gave them to *Ishpiniibin*. She held the young girl and told her of the lessons she'd learned during her vision quest, of how she'd dreamed her name.

The guests ate heartily to ensure plentiful times for the girl; they prayed for her long life and good health.[9] When the *Ojibway* religion was strong, people with supernatural powers were invited to naming feasts. One might give a tiny cane, to inspire long life; another a replica of a gun, to wish the child success as a hunter; another, a stone that held mystical forces. Each would give the child a name—a phrase—charged with meaning. The gifts would hang over the baby's cradle and would be explained to her each day when she played with them. As she grew older, she would be urged to seek blessings: visions granting power directly from her supernaturals.[10]

Each year, when the hills blaze with the colours of late summer, the story surfaces in *Ishpiniibin's* memory; the voice of her namer visits her, though the wise old woman is beyond this life in the Land of Souls. *Ishpiniibin* recalls the years of her childhood, when she followed Medicine Woman through the woods, when she was introduced to the plant world, and came to know their names and to learn their medicines.[11] In the abundant seasons, she knows the richness of her name, its power and character that will carry her through her time on earth. She takes gifts to Medicine Woman's burial place, and prays to the Great Spirit that her soul is content.

Through her life, the girl may be known by as many as six or seven names. As for all women, her names signify protection. For men, names are given that signify power. Her family has their own familiar name for her; girlfriends call her by a nickname. She has a name that denotes her totem, and a name that more than anything else, rings a pleasant sound.[12]

But there will be no *Wawiindaassowin* for the little girl *Ishpiniibin* holds in her arms. Nor did the baby's brothers live long enough to receive names and identities to prepare them for their journey.

"It is late little fawn," *Ishpiniibin* tells the little one. She rises and holds the wheezing bundle closer to her. "We must go to sleep so that tomorrow I can come back to collect the fish."

The lonesome call of a loon echoes across the bay, amplified in the silent, starry night. It reminds *Ishpiniibin* that some of her people are of his clan, that the loon is their totem. Her people also belong to the clans of the Muskrat, the Crow, the Beaver, the Crane and the Snake.[13] They are the survivors, remnants of the powerful *Mississaugas*—one of the bands of the *Ojibway* tribe—or *Chippewa,* that lived at the mouth of a river by that name. The name *Ojibway* was given to the people whose *makizinan* have puckered seams. They are people of the

Algonkin Nation.[14] Their lives follow the four seasons: *Mnookmig*—spring or sap season; *Niibin*—summer or the abundant season; *Dagwaagig*—autumn or the fading season, and *Bboon* winter, or cold freezing weather.[15]

Before the Hats and the Black Coat men came from across the Salt Water, her people's prayers to the four directions were answered. They prayed to Mother Earth beneath them for the gifts she provided. They prayed to *Chi Mnidoo*, the Great Spirit, who sleeps above Chi-gamiing—the Great Lake of the *Ojibway*.[16]

Before the silence, her people offered pipes of tobacco to the Sun; to *Waabnang*, Spirit of the East; to *Zhaawanang*, Spirit of the South; to *Bigishmog*, Spirit of the West, and to *Giiwednong*, Spirit of the North. They sought the favour of their own personal spirit guides, that they might live and prosper. They gave gifts of thanks to the spirits of all living plants and animals that shared Mother Earth with them.[17] Since the arrival of the Hats and the Black Coat men, many of their prayers to the Great Spirit and for all that the Creator provides, have gone as if unheard. The Black Coat men brought their own Creator, their own power.[18]

Outside the flap of the *wiigwaam, Ishpiniibin's* aunt tugs on the stitches of a legging for *Shawundais*. *Ishpiniibin* unwraps the child and goes inside the *wiigwaam* to place her beneath Grandmother's blanket. The old woman stirs long enough to fold the baby to her chest. Together they seek the comfort of sleep beneath animal robes, and will remain that way until sunrise.

The girl watches her aunt's nimble fingers draw strands of leather in and out of the soft mooseskin. *Ishpiniibin* thinks of her own mother, known for her intricate quill and beadwork. The most precious pieces of her work had been buried with her. *Ishpiniibin* arranges pieces of mooseskin on her lap and resumes work on a pair of *makizinan*[19] that her uncle will wear at the *mnoomin* harvest.

Lifeless sturgeon carpet the floors of the birchbark canoes. The women join their men now to take their harvest back to camp; their baskets brim with the limp largesse. One of the men offers a final gift of tobacco on the shore: the Fish Mnidoo was generous to them. The grandmothers tend the babies and small children back at camp. The other young ones who can keep the pace of the walk carry the remaining fish in their arms. The fish will provide a feast tonight, and what remains of it will be smoked and kept for the rice harvest and for the hunt. From the largest of the sturgeon, the bladders will be cured and used to store oil.[20]

When the canoes are emptied, the men hoist the vessels over their heads, and lead the way up the trail. The women follow, backs bent with the weight of the baskets.[21] The air resonates with the sounds of bees, birds and insects: sounds that soon will be silenced by winter. Birds gather in the trees along the trail, chattering plans of migration.

The fishing party hears voices carried to them on the breeze: voices that are not speaking Indian, but a different sound: one that *Ishpiniibin* does not understand. At the brow of the hill, the footpath crosses a trail used by the Hats and their horses. Three black specks bob on the horizon, their melodious voices clear on the wind.

Shawundais slows his pace, and lowers his canoe to the ground. The rest of the group waits. The black specks grow, their voices swelling as they come nearer. The Hats follow: some on horseback, others in wagons, still more on foot. Their voices unite with the three Black Coat men on horseback. When the choralling group reaches the fishing party, one of the Black Coats dismounts and approaches *Shawundais*. They appear to know each other; their hands extend to touch, to grasp the other. The Black Coat tries to speak Indian; he gestures to the west in large, sweeping motions. His hands join together under his chin and point upwards. *Ishpiniibin* has seen her uncle make this sign at times. The Black Coat's eyes close; then he includes all of the fishing party in a mimic embrace.

Shawundais nods and points in the direction of their camp, gestures to all of his people and points beyond: the way the Black Coat is headed. The fishing party continues along the footpath; the transient voices of the Hats and Black Coats gain volume. The Hat women pass *Ishpiniibin*; their long cloth dresses sweep the ground. Their heads are covered with the same skins the colours of flowers. She fondles her worn deerskin shift, then lifts the swollen, dripping basket and continues along the path. When they reach camp, *Ishpiniibin* and the young women busy the children while the older women cook.

Shawundais is near the fire. As soon as they'd arrived back, he'd left with a basket of fish in hand, in the direction of the Hats' settlement. When he returned, a bottle had replaced the basket. He now lies by the sputtering fire, with a belly full of whiskey. He tosses back what remains in the bottle. *Shawundais* knows firewater, how it can deaden his feelings of sadness. Since his two boys died, he has been troubled and confused. He often seeks comfort in firewater. He crumples beside the fire; the echoing sounds from the distant clearing wash over him. They hadn't gone to the camp meeting like he'd promised the Black Coat man, but the voices have found him anyway. The voices continue through the night. *Shawundais* soberly listens to words he can feel the power of but whose meaning he cannot grasp. He cries out, clutching his breaking heart. He knows that the white people are talking to their Great Spirit, but he is unable to join them.

Shawundais remembers times of plenty, when beaver were abundant, and his people trapped, and sold many pelts, when they wore silver brooches and earrings, when they draped themselves in cloth the colour of blood and carried *wampum*.[21a] But then the furtraders came. With them they brought *Shkiniwaaboo*, and when his people drank it, they acted like blind men.

Now there are no more beaver; the furtraders have gone west, and with them the *Mnidoo*.[22] Since the time *Shawundais* had been a warrior for the Great Father across the Salt Lake, he and his people continued to receive gifts from the Red Coats.[23] Indian people are swift runners. They know the four directions, the movements of every living thing, and how to abide by the four seasons. With the Great Father's warriors they had fought against the Blue Coats south of *On-Tar-ack*.[24] The Great Father promised to show his gratitude forever, but now he is giving their hunting ground to the Hats. The great forest is gone now, further than the eye can see. Skinned and dressed, the trees now stand as houses and barns; their stumps line great patches of bald land, and animals are kept there, driving the deer and moose further north—with *Shawundais* and his people in their pursuit.

The Indian people have struggled to remain; they have tried to live with the Hats, who claim to be friends. Until the Black Coat men came into the woods *Shawundais* saw only the Hats, who needed his guidance. These people wanted his knowledge of hunting, of fishing, of plants for eating, and for medicines. But now his people are called savage pagans and they are prevented from crossing fenced land. More Hats continue to come. Now these people would sooner give shelter to their animals than to *Shawundais* and his people. Fences keep the animals in and the Indians out.

The British army had worn red coats and carried rifles with bayonets. They'd dragged fire-breathing iron horses through the fields. Now the soldiers he meets wear black and carry books. They say another Great Father will save them. The Black Coats say the ways of the medicine men are evil and their spirits damned.

Ishpiniibin wakens early, but not before Grandmother, who is up each day before the sun. The girl feels a fullness in her belly. She rises up from the skins and finds blood smeared on her lean dark thighs, on the blanket covering her cedar pallet. Grandmother comes to the flap of the *wiigwaam*, as if she'd been waiting for *Ishbiniibin* to awaken.

"You will begin your fast now, *Ishpiniibin*. You are a new woman among us. In these times, your body has powerful medicine, and at every moon your medicine will be a threat to the unborn, the young, yes—all living things. You will spend these times away from us, in the moon lodge, each time until the flow passes. I will teach you, for I am past my moons and your medicine cannot harm me."

Grandmother shrouds *Ishpiniibin* in an old dress. The old woman crouches over the dead coals of the night's fire and pulls a charred stick from it that she pounds into powder and smears around the girl's eyes and forehead.

" Look down in these times, my granddaughter. Do not cast your eyes on any living thing. Your power is a blight and we will all suffer from your actions".

Grandmother leads her through the camp, scattering leaves behind *Ishpiniibin's* path, a warning to men, pregnant women and babies, that there is a menstruating woman in the moon lodge.

Inside the moon lodge, another young woman sits beading mooseskin leggings. Grandmother removes a bag from her shoulder and places it in front of *Ishpiniibin*. In it there is a body scratcher to keep her from contaminating herself should she need to calm a skin irritation. She has brought *makizinan* for her to bead, and a skirt to mend.[25]

"I will come tomorrow and bring food for you, granddaughter. Now you must sit quietly and think about what it is to become a woman." When Grandmother leaves the lodge, the other young woman looks up from her work and chuckles.

"Do not think too hard about the food your grandmother promises," says the girl as she leans back and stretches. "It will be tired old scraps that even hungry dogs wouldn't touch."

Ishpiniibin works on her *makizinan* and talks with her lodge mate who has been fasting for three days. She tells *Ishpiniibin* that one night young men had tried to get into their lodge.

"What did you do? " *Ishpiniibin's* mind races. She sees herself as the young woman; she freezes with fear, but is soon relieved when she hears her lodgemate laugh.

"I covered my eyes with one hand, and turned round and round and round. I held my other arm out, so that when they came near me, I hit them. I threw *zaasgan*;[26] I threw the tired old food, anything my hands touched. Ha! They knew I was not an easy target, and left as quickly as they came."

Ishpiniibin tires of her work but Grandmother has told her that she must work hard in the moon lodge, that the commitment and effort she spends there will bode well for her life as a mature woman.[27]

Hunger gnaws and growls in the pit of her stomach. She curls up on the floor of the lodge, and soon both young women are asleep. *Ishpiniibin* dreams that young men come into the lodge again. She, too, covers her eyes, but she has a stick, and as she whirls around she hears the men cry out as the stick makes contact with their flesh. They retreat.

In another dream, *Ishpiniibin* is once again in the moon lodge. There are more young women with her. Behind the flaps of the lodge, they create an intricate new dance that one woman dreamed during her time there. *Ishpiniibin* feels the power of their dance, the strength and youth the women have as they circle the fire. She feels her heartbeat and the drum throbbing in unison. The women all wear the same beaded dresses, all patterned from designs that came to them during moon lodge dreams.[28]

The night is long and *Ishpiniibin* grows restless. She hears the other young woman talking in a low voice, facing the wall of the lodge, away from her. *Ishpiniibin* raises herself up on her fists, quietly, to look at the covered mass lying across from her. No one else is there.

" What do you say? Who do you talk to?"

" To this young man here. He leaves now to ask my mother and father if he may marry me. But I know my parents won't let him, because he came to me here in the moon lodge". The young woman rolls over and slips into a deep, silent sleep once again.

Outside, the Northern Lights splash across the late night sky. Before Medicine Woman passed on, she told *Ishpiniibin* to watch for them: there she would see Medicine Woman, her mother and father—all her departed relations—dancing joyfully.[29] The sky is lively, but all is silent. She knows that there has been no young suitor in their lodge.

Ishpiniibin follows her lodge mate to the dreaming place. She is comfortable there. She feels no hunger. Medicine Woman meets her on the path to the dreaming place. *Ishpiniibin* has grown to become a young woman, but Medicine Woman is no older than the day she passed on to the Land of Souls. They are in the forest beyond the summer camp, collecting plants. She sings the medicine chant, and offers the medicine prayer.[30]

Medicine Woman turns back the leaves of a sumac tree to reveal the work of a spider: the web is shaped like the petals of a flower. The stamen: a morning dew drop, glistening hostage to the afternoon sun. When morning comes, *Ishpiniibin* remembers the dream; with a stick she traces the outline of the flower on the floor of the lodge. She pulls the skirt from her mending bag. Holes gape down the length of the garment, the lacing ragged in places, or completely bare. She smoothes the skirt on the floor beside the sketch of the petal. At the bottom of the bag she finds moosehide laces wrapped around a bone needle. With the pointed end pressed firmly into a corner of the skirt near the side seam, she copies, impressing the flower on her skirt. She wets the needle with her saliva to soften the nap of the mooseskin. Coloured beads pattern her mind's eye.[31]

Grandmother appears at the entrance to the lodge with a sack and her weaving frame. She squats and places the contents of the bag in front of her granddaughter: a rock-hard *zaasgan*, sticks of dried meat tougher than wood chips, and a piece of rancid fish. *Ishpiniibin* nods and lifts a piece of meat to her lips. She sucks it; a branch of the maple tree has more flavour, she thinks.

Grandmother settles on the floor across from *Ishpiniibin*. On her lap lies a weaving frame, beside her, a rope of rabbit fur.[32] She takes up the strips and settles to a rhythmic drawing in and out, gently tugging the pieces of soft pelt into a square. Laced together, many squares will make a blanket, like the one *Ishpiniibin's* mother gave her when she was a young girl. She remembers rubbing the down-like fur across her face at night when she waited for sleep to take her. She wants it now, to lie down with it, while she listens to her Grandmother tell a story.

Her voice is deep and mesmerizing when she recounts the legend of *Shingibis*, the hell-diver,

> *"Two girls wanted to hunt each a man (i.e., to marry). So they set out on a journey. When they got to a lake they saw a man in a little boat, and asked him who he was. He said he was Wamigisakon, and that he was their pearl beads. Then they told him to come after them and put them in his boat. They got into the boat and went on until they came to a village. When it became night he said to the girls, "Get me my belt, there is going to be a dance". So they gave him his belt, which was really only basswood bark which he got from the shore. He put his belt on, and the girls went with him to the place where the dance was to be held. When they got to the door nobody knew the poor fellow, who had said he was Wamigisakon. He was only Shingibis, the hell-diver, trying to make believe that he was Wamigisakon. However, the girls went in, and they saw the chief of the place, Wamigisakon, the great pearl chief, full of pearl beads. The girls stayed there all night. There were very many girls there, for Wamigisakon wanted to get married and so had all the girls in the room dance before him. He put a mark on the one he had chosen, and her parents, when she came home, examined her clothes, found the mark, and knew she was to be Wamigisakon's wife. The girl chosen was the grandchild of an old woman. The two girls had no luck that night. They left the Shingibis, but never came to any good".* [33]

At the end of her fifth day in the moon lodge, *Ishpiniibin*'s flow stops completely. When Grandmother arrives, she brings with her a bladder of water so *Ishpiniibin* can bathe and put on the new gown her grandmother has made for her. In new clothes, *Ishpiniibin* shares hot corn soup with Grandmother. The taste runs wild in the young woman's mouth; the old woman scorns *Ishpiniibin*'s eagerness. [34] They return to the camp at sundown, where all the grandmothers have prepared a seasonal ceremony for *Ishpiniibin* and her lodge mate. They offer prayers and sacrificial food to the rice *mnidoo* and to the fish *mnidoo*, the foods of the season, that they may see fit to forgive the new women, to allow them to eat fresh food at the time of their moons. They pray to the spirit of evil womanhood that the rest of the tribe be spared any contamination by their actions. That the new women will continue to observe all other customs of the moon lodge. The ceremony ends in a feast. Grandmother stands beside *Ishpiniibin*.

"When the ceremonies end after the cycle of the seasons, you will be given a new name to have during this moon time". Grandmother nudges *Ishpiniibin*. "Then you will be ready to take a husband".[35]

Grandmother smiles, but *Ishpiniibin* senses a confusion in the old woman's face: a look she has never before seen. Grandmother becomes silent. Later, *Ishpiniibin* learns that *Shawundais* has been to a camp meeting. He has been with the Black Coat men, listening to them sing and talk with their Creator. There, he learned that Christians need to be baptized or they cannot go to the white man's heaven when they die.

Ishpiniibin does not know that Grandmother has seen him crying, helpless and alone in the woods, but in their lodge, *Ishpiniibin* has heard him call out—many times—in the night. She remains silent to the dream he has recounted when he escapes from his tormented sleep.

Ishpiniibin remains silent, but shares her uncle's fear when she awakens the following morning to learn that while her family slept, Little Fawn had passed on to the Land of Souls. Tears darken the earth that her uncle scrapes and claws, sobbing and moaning, while he prepares the child's grave. While his wife tucks her baby in her bundleboard, Grandmother hovers, waiting to fasten Little Fawn's rattle onto the frame. The old woman wails in unison with her daughter as they rock back and forth over their departed little girl.

Ishpiniibin gathers bark from a fallen birch and four strong sticks from the woods beyond their camp. She drives the sticks into the ground at the four corners of the small grave. They place Little Fawn there with her head in the west. Her favourite blanket is draped over the bundleboard before Shawundais pushes the earth over his daughter's body. *Ishpiniibin* rests the birchbark on the stakes, protection against the rain. They offer tobacco to *Chi Mnidoo* and pray that Little Fawn will travel well to the Land of Souls.

Seated around the grave, they share a pudding made from *mnoomin*, a food the baby has never known. They tell her stories of this special food, encouraging her to eat before she leaves them.[35a]

"You remember the *mnoomin* harvest, Little Fawn," Ishpiniibin speaks softly, "You watched from your little nest in the willow tree while we parched the rice..." she recalls.

In *Mnoomnii Giizis*—the Grain Moon, or Indian Summer, *mnoomin* is gathered. *Mnoomin—Mnidoo g'tigaan*—from the Great Spirit's garden—is sacred, a food that is respected like the *mnidoos*, and one *Shawundais* and his people have planted for many generations, in the four directions of their wandering.

Before the silence, *Ishpiniibin's* people numbered many and the chiefs and principal men led large tribes. In those days, the chief would prepare a leather pouch of tobacco and go to the lodge of an elder. When given permission to enter, he would disappear behind the flap. Inside, he asked the elder—his most esteemed rice harvester, to prepare for the harvest. The elder accepted the gift of tobacco, and an invitation to eat his first meal of the day at the chief's fire.

They would offer tobacco at the water's edge—for the Spirit of *Mnoomin* before the elder climbed into a waiting canoe. A young man poled the elder through marshes as he gathered grains of rice from each bay where it grew. In late afternoon, the elder returned to camp, and together, into a steaming iron pot he placed the rice gathered from all the bays. When it was cooked, each harvester would eat from the pot, and pray that this harvest would provide them with sufficient rice to sustain them through *Bboon*—the season of cold, freezing weather.[36]

In early morning light, canoes gather in the cove. Like all the other couples, *Shawundais* poles, guiding his woman into the bays, to gather the rice. The first grains of the harvest are placed with tobacco on the water, and a prayer of thanksgiving is offered to the Great Spirit, for the plentiful rice before them.

With a cedar stick in each hand, the women bend the rice stalks into the canoes, and thresh the ripe grain free from the stalks. The women's motions are even, rhythmic; grain gently showers the bottom of the canoes. A seasoned harvester loses none to the lake; the rice is clean and free from stalks. The ricers return to shore in late afternoon, their canoes half-filled to the gunnels. Fires had been stoked all day; *zaasgan*, corn soup, ducks and fish were ready for the feast. Large wooden bowls filled with steaming rice pudding—hoarded from the previous harvest, are presented for this occasion. By nightfall, pickers from across the lake join the others to celebrate, drumming and dancing long into the night.[37]

The harvest is spread on blankets to dry in the sun for the next few days. Crickets and wasps arrive to clean the grains of tiny worms that live on rice plants. When it is dry and free of worms, the green rice is parched—stirred with a paddle in iron pots over slow, closely watched fires. The kernels release steam, and turn from green to gold to dark brown, the women all the while turning the contents of the hissing cauldrons. The men don new *makizinan* to dance—to loosen the husks from the black rice. Pans of danced rice are held over the pots, and with help from offshore breezes, the lighter chaff blows away—winnowing—from the heavier rice that drops back into the pots.

Early snow powders the trail that *Shawundais* and his people follow north. The men carry canoes, and where the river bends and forms bays, they float them, piled high with branches. Like newly formed islands, beneath this foliage they drift closer to the *zhiishiib*, the first gifts of the hunting season.[38] *Shawundais* remembers times, when returning to camp at night they would offer thanks to the Great Spirit—when the fire received the first fowl that had been shot, the hunters would sing songs, in appreciation for the gifts.

By torchlight the men paddle silently toward the *waawaashkesh* that come to feed in the rice beds. The stillness of the cool night air explodes with the report of a single rifle shot. The deer collapses—water splashing, and falls into the rushes at the edge of the rice bed. The men drag it to shore where they disembowel and clean the fruits of the hunt.

"All birds do I feed" was an expression they said, before the silence, when the deer's blood was tossed in the four directions, in gratitude.[39]

In the morning, the women retrieve the carcass and set to work on it. At camp, *Ishpiniibin's* aunt skins the animal, and cuts the venison into pieces to cook or to dry. She watches as her aunt draws precise strokes between the animal's muscle and bone, separating the fibrous sinew that when dried will be used for sewing; the animal's large organs will be cured to hold food.[40]

The women carry the skins to winter camp; plunged under the ice of the frozen lake, the skins will soak for two weeks to remove the hair and later, in *Nmebine Giizis*—Sucker Moon, the skins will be tanned.[41] It is a time when *Ishpiniibin* and the other young women gather wood and silently observe their grandmothers, appreciative of the knowledge they have to share. *Ishpiniibin* recalls other Sucker Moons, the smoke rising up around Grandmother who tended the slow-burning fires, turned the skins, giving more smoke or less, to alter the shades of the hides.

Shawundais and his wife begin the hunt together. She keeps a watchful eye for danger, while *Shawundais* focuses down the barrel of his rifle. If the hunt is fruitful, she will return with the kill, while *Shawundais* continues to hunt, returning to camp only when he is successful. At camp, they will eat what his wife brings back, but at each meal, her husband's portion will be carefully stored. When he returns, the women prepare a feast; his wife removes and mends his clothes and gives him tobacco to smoke. In better times, with a full belly, he would sing praises to his *mnidoo* for his good fortune. At first light, he will leave again.[42]

When storms keep them near the fire, *Shawundais* and his wife make snowshoes from ash saplings they have gathered. *Shawundais* bends and slashes and shapes oval wooden frames into which his wife weaves webs of mooseskin lacing.

Smoke ascends skyward through the opening in the *wiigwaam*. When ice and snow cover Mother Earth and the days are dark, *Ishpiniibin* draws close to the hot stones next to the fire with all her relations. Little ones lie with their heads in mothers' or grandmothers' laps. They dare not stir, eager to hear every word the Elders say. *Ishpiniibin* savours the fragrant smoke rising from the men's pipes, a mixture of tobacco and sumach that reminds her of past *Mnidoo giizis,* when she first listened to the legends of her people.[43] She never tires of the stories. Some legends make even the most serious relations laugh long and loud until it appears the *wiigwaam* will burst from their convulsions.

> " As Nanebozho [Nenaboozhoo] was walking on a
> sandy shore he felt hungry. It was now in autumn.
> He saw an object moving towards him. He saw
> that the object was a bear. He pulled up a sappling
> [sic] and prepared to club the bear when he came

near, so he hid himself. When the bear came near enough he made a jump towards him and with one blow killed the bear. He built a fire and singed the hair off, opened and roasted the bear. When sufficiently roasted he cut the meat up in fine pieces, intending to eat leisurely. Before he commenced eating, a squeaking noise of a tree annoyed him, and to destroy the noise he climbed up the tree. While endeavouring to separate the split crotch of the tree his hand was caught in it. While he was working to get his hand out, a pack of wolves ran down to the shore and they came towards him; this made him work more to extricate his hand. The wolves began eating his intended meal, taking no heed to Nanebozho's shouting to scare them. When the wolves eat[sic] up all the meat, Nanebozho got his hand out of the crotched tree and came down. He found nothing left for him to eat except the brain in the skull which he could not get out. He said, " I will transform myself into a little snake and enter the skull to eat the brain." He did so, and when he got through eating he could not get out of the skull. Nanebozho walked along the shore without seeing and at last fell into the lake and swam under the surface of the water. When he came up to the surface he heard voices saying, "there is a bear swimming, let us kill him". There was a chase on the lake and the parties came up and struck the bear on its head and split it open and Nanebozho jumped out and got to the dry land."[44]

Another Elder takes up the Eagle feather and begins the legend of how Ishpiniibin's people received the gift of Corn.

"Many winters ago, the Great Spirit appeared to one of our wise forefathers, and showed him a plant of the Mundahmin,[mnoomin] or the Indians' corn, on which grew two ears. The Great Spirit then told him to preserve the two ears until the next spring, when he was to plant them. He was further commanded to preserve the whole crop, and send two ears to each of the surrounding nations, with *the injunction that they were not to eat of it until the third crop. The wise Indian did as he was commanded. His corn grew strong and brought forth much. The next summer he enlarged his ground, and planted all his seed, which yielded plentifully. He then sent two ears to each of the surrounding tribes, with proper directions, which they observed, and by this means the corn was distributed among all the American Indians. It is considered by them the best grain in the world, because the Great Spirit gave it to them for their bread."*[45]

The small ones sit wide-eyed, clutching their mothers' skirts when an elder recounts the Land of the Little Crane Men. It is the land of the unknown, where little girls are taken, kidnapped from the woods near their camp. This, the children are told, is the reason why little girls should always stay close to home.[46]

"Aaho." In unison, the fathers acknowledge their concern.

By the cold, harsh season of *Mnidoo giizis—Mnidoo* moon— there is nothing to eat. The stores of dried meat, rice, maple sugar and berries have been depleted for some time. They share a crumbling bone and tree bark from which they make broth. The Great Spirit they once prayed to cannot hear them against the howling wind.

It is a time of uneasiness: when gales and endless snows threaten a visit from *Windigo*.[47] Her family dares not utter the name of this evil spirit that prowls the forest, who waits to visit one of them when they are weakened by hunger. Under the power of *Windigo*, a victim will prey on his own family. *Ishpiniibin* fights to keep the haunting dreams out of the *wiigwaam*. She and her people know that through dreams and visions of this deadly creature, he is able to make his victims *Windigo*. If he is hungry enough—starving—he begins to crave human flesh. His victims suffer from the same hunger. *Windigo* becomes a beaver, and when they try to kill him, they become *Windigo*.

The earth groans and the lodge trembles as a hulking skeleton of ice approaches. *Ishpiniibin* sees a muskrat at the edge of the forest staggering towards the camp. Its paws are webbed, and like a floundering duck, the rodent pushes itself along the frozen ground, flapping the useless appendages away from its body. *Ishpiniibin* wakens, relieved it is only a dream, as the animal turns toward her *wiigwaam*.[48]

There is no trust during the time of *Windigo*, when enemies' sorcerers can send starvation to a camp. Weather can be changed through sorcery. It can force game away, and if that happens, the starving victims become *Windigo*. There was a time when *Ishpiniibin* and her people prayed to the Great Spirit for strength to overcome the power of Windigo. Now, sick and starving, they lie near the fire, moaning when the wind whips the *wiigwaam*, when the trees creak and groan under its force.

With dawn's first light, twelve members from another band arrive at *Shawundais'* camp. The men have brought fish to share, but when *Shawundais* and his people sit down to devour the food, one of the twelve tells him that they must pray, that they have the Black Coats' God to thank for this food. Thanks must be given to God that their bellies will be filled. The twelve men kneel and lead *Shawundais* in prayer.

Shawundais and his people listen to these men who met the Creator through a Black Coat—an *Anishnaabeg*[49]— who speaks their own tongue. All men—*Anishnaabeg* and white men—are brothers, says the Black Coat. The Creator makes one man, and out of this man, all people come—black, white, yellow, red— different colours because they live in the different seasons of the four directions, he says. What the Creator promises for one man, he promises for all, he says. The Creator loves them all the same, he says.[50]

The visitors invite *Shawundais* to go with them, to meet their Creator. *Ishpiniibin* listens to them promise her uncle an end to hunger, hope for his people. She gathers the empty bowls from the men as they rise to leave. She will clean the bowls, but there is nothing more to put in them. She watches her uncle, stooped and weary, follow the men out of the camp.

Upper Canada: The Self-Conscious Society

In 1763, more than fifty years before *Ishbiniibin's* birth, a country called Britain ruled all this place called Canada. Twenty years later, the area known as New York State—traditionally occupied by Six Nations tribes—would become territory of another country to the south, called the United States. The Iroquoian Six Nations wanted to remain with the British, but they needed a home. At the same time, land had to be found for the United Empire Loyalists who wanted to come north as well.

In 1783, all of the north shore of the St. Lawrence River above Montreal and along the north shore of Lake Ontario to Niagara was surveyed. The first township laid out in Upper Canada that year was called Kingston.[51] By the following year, 3,686 Loyalists populated the area. In 1791, there were 14,000, and Upper Canada—the older part, and Lower Canada were created. By 1812, there were 90,000 people in the township and three out of five were Americans.[52]

Since the War of 1812, Upper Canada had become a "self-conscious" society. American ideologies were no longer trusted—including American Methodism, the religion to which *Ishpiniibin's* people would convert. Since 1794, Methodist Society circuits in Canada were under an American jurisdiction called the New York Conference, and in 1810, the Upper Canada District became part of the Genesee Conference, also based in the United States. But when the conference was held in July, 1812, no Canadian itinerants—travelling preachers—were permitted to cross the American border to attend.[53]

Within three years, the immigration policy changed, and 17,000 Euroamericans emigrated to Upper Canada. In less than five years, the only land left in the area of Bay of Quinte to Kingston was in the geographical backwaters. Government administration and its policies continued to shift with the influx of settlers.

The demographic profile of Upper Canada was changing rapidly. The new immigrants wanted land. They loathed the

Indians and the "philanthropic benevolent Home Government."[54] *Ishpiniibin's* people, the "savage" children, had become a smudge on the landscape. Until now, the British government and its governors had been operating informally with the Indians, like strangers dancing: nervous and tentative, yet polite. Very rapidly, the government's "backwoods diplomacy"—their style of dealing with the Indians, evolved to become the Indian Policy.

A blueprint for Upper Canada had been in place in Lower Canada since the mid-17th century under the Jesuits, and in the United States as well, where the idea of turning the Indians into farmers and taking their land, was a policy put in place by Thomas Jefferson.[55] In the United States, trading houses were promoted, where Indians could buy dry goods, farming supplies and implements. When the Indians owed more than they were able to pay, it was thought that they would trade even more land, to settle their accounts.[56]

The British government purchased land along the Grand River (that flows into Lake Erie) from the *Mississaugas* for the Iroquois. But there was one group of Mohawks of the Iroquois Confederacy that wanted to live in the Bay of Quinte area on Lake Ontario. Something had to be done for them; consequently, two hundred square miles—from Ganonoque to the Trent River, and north 36 miles from Lake Ontario—was purchased from the *Mississaugas*.[57] Payment was hunting munitions and enough cloth to make a dozen coats. No annuity was included in the deal—no annual payments of either ammunition or supplies, not even a determined sum to be paid to each member of the tribe, as was customary. The *Mississaugas* had lived in the Kingston area for close to 100 years, but now had no right to be there.[58]

Between 1790 and 1812, seventy-six Methodist missionaries were sent to Canada, "most of whom were of a humble and social background and few had been extensively educated."[59] Theological degrees weren't a priority for eighteenth century Methodism which thrived on the highly emotional experiences of its converts. The leaders were attentive to messages they received from dreams and visions. Singing and praying were present in all Methodist worship.[60] Methodism promoted temperance and the simple way of life; its doctrine was salvation through the redemption of sin. The Methodist Movement sought converts in Upper Canada through travelling preachers—circuit riders, or itinerant ministers: the Black Coat Men. Appealing to settlers, they held camp meetings—religious sessions that went on for days, attracting thousands to clearings in the woods.

Upper Canada needed an established church, but the Methodists had little hope of gaining favour as a choice. At that time, it was government policy that only the wealthy, educated and well-bred should govern. Government wanted an Established Church for the country, and its connection with the United Kingdom had to be preserved and unchanged.[61] The Methodists got caught up in the controversy that the Church of England was to be the Established Church of Upper Canada.

The Big Black Coat Man

Chi-Makdewkonye—the Big Black Coat Man— was known to most white people as Elder William Case of the Methodist Episcopal Church. Brother Case. Father Case. Passionate to his calling and to the challenges of the frontier, he believed that God would provide for all. His dreams were fraught with messages and he believed they prophesied things to come.

His recurring dream—of gathering the Indians together— weighed profound. He was as new to the Indians and their ways as they were to him and the ways of his church. But the Indians were grateful for the new direction, and hopeful that this new religion would provide them with strength. In the church's care, Case saw them transform into cultured people— without the coarse, immoral ways of the emotional settlers.

Missionaries did the double-duty of performing services and of tending their flocks—by day and by night. Upper Canada was missionary territory and it was their responsibility to get The Word into every destitute settlement. They were exhorters of

> *"... peace and the support of the civil authorities. They were to encourage the establishment of Sabbath Schools, to recommend economy, decency and industry, to press the worship of God in every family,—to visit the sick and assist to the poor—to administer the ordinances—to labour for and to suffer with their flocks, and to do all in their power to bring sinners to repentance, and thereby endeavor to extend the interests of the Redeemer's Kingdom."[62]*

This was all to be done on horseback, in the four seasons of the Lord, in the wilderness of the New World.

The first Methodist services had been held on the upper St. Lawrence River, and later in the Bay of Quinte, where the first chapel was built at Hay Bay in 1792. The area would remain Methodist territory for the next hundred years. Until 1828, there was very little funding for the erection of churches. Markets, stuffy kitchens and noisy taverns were the usual sites of prayer meetings.[63] The first camp meeting was arranged in the Bay of Quinte circuit in 1805 by Henry Ryan and William Case. Their teamwork was inspiring. Before a Methodist Society existed there, Kingston Town had been a rowdy port, populated with "very irreligious" folk.

Ryan and Case used the local public market house for their chapel. It was hard work, rousing the cynics. When they rode into town, they tied their horses at an inn's hitching post, then arm in arm, they'd sing their way down the streets. More often than not the pious carollers began with 'Come let us march to Zion's Hill.' They drew attention to themselves, but that was their idea. By the time they reached the market-place, a large assembly was milling, and enveloped them. As a team, Ryan usually preached and Case would be his side-man, exhorting. Ryan was a powerful singer, and as a speaker, his voice could be heard through the town, and across the harbour. They were both a curiosity and an entertainment, accepted by most. What was bothersome was the lowlife—folks who tried to upset them from their butcher's block podium. It was a challenge to keep their lighting system operating when members of their congregation either snuffed their candles, or used them to singe the preachers' hair.[64]

Love feasts were simple meals highly seasoned with spiritual testimonials. These feasts and camp meetings drew settlers from as far as one hundred miles away, where they'd stay four or more days, at these emotionally charged religious festivals. The natural setting, combined with all of the appealing qualities of the Methodist doctrine, attracted the Native population too. It sounded like the answer to their problems: it promised respite from hardship, a pure life from the influence of alcohol, and everlasting life with the Great Father.

Camp meetings proceeded like extended religious services, with several ministers each giving a sermon, followed by prayer meetings, where everyone was invited to urge repenting sinners over the brink, to pray for them and for each other. To direct that much energy, to focus on individuals and their well-being, was powerful to witness, to experience.

Passion charged these marathon religious orgies, where any time for doubt or introspection was filled with more testimony from others who'd just found God. Every waking hour—and no doubt dreamtime—was saturated with religion.

Only Presiding Elders—senior officials—and their preachers were allowed to organize camp meetings. This decision weeded out the influence of preachers who threatened hell and damnation, or who used mass hypnotism, or preyed upon the weakened physical and emotional states of the people to secure their converts. Camp meetings were for the "revival and renewal of life", never intended to replace itinerant preachers or circuit riders.

Methodist societies were formed with a hierarchy of a local preacher, exhorters and class leaders. It was the class leader's responsibility to keep an eye on each one of his class members— at least once a week, to make sure they were on spiritual track.

Class meetings were instructional sessions that focussed on the religious and moral precepts of Methodism. The preachers conducted quarterly examinations to probe the state of members' souls. The practice of intercession—to plead in prayer for another person—was a very important aspect of religion for the Indians, who thought that no one cared about them—let alone intercede on their behalf.[65]

Settlers like Susanna Moodie regarded camp meetings as part of their popular culture, much like barn-raisings or quilting or haying bees. They were *pure* diversion from the drudge of trying to tame the new landscape. These marathon revival meetings were emotionally cathartic to some, and brought about behavioural changes in people that led them to the security of the Methodist Society and of its doctrine—all of which led to a change in their moral and ethical standards.[66]

In 1824, there was a complete separation of Canadian ministers from the Methodist Episcopal Church of the United States, and a separate annual conference was established for Canada. When the first session of the Canada Conference of the Methodist Episcopal Church was held in Hallowell (Picton) on August 25, 1824, William Case succeeded Henry Ryan as Presiding Elder of the Bay Of Quinte District. He was transferred from Upper Canada District, and became deeply devoted to the spiritual wellbeing of the *Mississaugas* in the Belleville and Kingston area.[67]

The Methodists' work with the Indians played on the heartstrings of several social strata. Newspapers and religious periodicals featured reports regularly. Methodism appealed to the common man, to the helpless and to the hopeless, and to the converted—who gave the church money. Many Indians gratefully tossed onto the collection plate their silver brooches, armbands and ear and nose-bobs which were then sold to jewellers to further the cause.[68]

The Lord's Way was not without struggle for the Big Black Coat Man, and times of emotional depression often clouded his mind. He was passing through middle age unwed, and when he finally found young Hetty – Hester Ann Hubbard, a pious young woman from New York, she was taken from him two years later. Mrs. Case had been victim to a lingering mental illness that had hastened its hold on her with the birth of their baby girl. They'd christened her Eliza Jane, after their friend, who would later become Case's second wife.

Case often thought about the conversion of Chief *Kahkewaquonaby*—whom they now called Peter Jones. It was an event that had turned the Church—to which the young Indian man had given himself, his life—in a new direction. Case was Presiding Elder at that camp meeting where he witnessed Jones' conversion. Case saw before him the role model—the leader they needed to convert the *Ojibway* nation: Peter Jones was a chief; he spoke *Ojibway*, as well as some English, and he had become a Christian.[69] Case knew the value of this Indian's religious passion and invited Jones to come and visit the *Mississaugas* and Mohawks in the Bay of Quinte area that winter.

Kahkewaquonaby

Kahkewaquonaby—Sacred Feathers—was the son of *Ojibway* mother, *Thubenahneequay,* and of Welsh father, Augustus Jones, a government surveyor. When he was born in 1802 at Burlington Heights, his parents wanted him to have all the privileges that white people enjoyed. At the age of 18, *Kahkewaquonaby* was baptized Peter Jones in the Anglican Church.[70]

He may have enjoyed a better life as an Anglican, but claims he continued to be the same wild Indian youth until he attended a five-day Methodist camp meeting in June, 1823, in Ancaster Township. Peter felt overwhelmed by the thousand-odd people who sang and prayed together in the religious campground day after day that summer. The presence of the Lord was there in the fields; he felt sure. But he felt sick, not joyful, and was too embarrassed to tell any one.

Kahkewaquonaby understood the words the Black Coats spoke: strong and full of love. They were words that made his heart swell. At times he felt he understood too much, and was sure they were talking about him. He felt miserable, helpless, and longed to be "saved". He wept at the thought of who he was, of what he'd done, and of his embarrassing emotions. He tried to hide his tears, but then saw that he wasn't the only one to display emotions. Others—white settlers, were "waking up" around him. They, too, were emotional—laughing or crying, or blissfully mesmerized.

His spiritual pain became unbearable, but he was afraid to ask to be prayed for. In the darkness he went into the woods by himself to pray. He knelt by a fallen tree; even the sound of leaves rustling made him uneasy. Deep in the forest, he "wrestled with God in prayer", and decided to return to the camp meeting and ask them to pray with him. When he reached the campground, he couldn't proceed and, as if they were reading his mind, someone arrived to take him into a prayer session. To pray for *him.* He was moved to tears that he, a "poor Indian," an "outcast," was included in the white man's religious world— and that more than one minister would speak to the Lord on his behalf.

His heart was filled with many different feelings that left him exhausted and confused. When he first started to pray, he wept, and his "heart was soft and tender." Later, it became "hard as stone." He felt that when he couldn't lift his head up—that there was no use; he was headed for hell. He left the prayer meeting at midnight and went to sleep in his tent.

The young Indian man was conspicuous in his absence and two ministers hunted for him to report that his sister had just been saved; he must join her. Peter hadn't known that his sister *wanted* to be saved, and now she was ahead of him on the Path. The preachers took him to his deliriously happy sister, who encouraged him—exhorted him—to be saved. By morning, he joined in her new-found joy.

The world appeared different to him and he was no longer shy to pray among the white people. "There was a time when I thought that the white man's God was never intended to be our God.......Christianity has found us and has lifted us up out of a horrible pit...and put a new song into our mouths...." [71]

Peter Jones committed to what became a 33-year career of missionary work among his people. Between 1825 and 1833, he translated the Lord's Prayer, the books of Genesis and Psalms, a vocabulary and a dictionary from English to Ojibway. [72]

> *"Their physical, intellectual and moral condition at that time was extremely low and miserable, darkness covered their minds, hunger and whiskey destroyed their health, wicked and designing men took advantage of their ignorance and their weaknesses, and they were fast dying off from the face of that magnificent country which their forefathers once proudly called their own",* he wrote in History of the Ojebway [sic] People. [73]

Within two years of Jones' conversion, more than half the Credit Band at the Grand River were members of the Methodist Church. He immediately established a mission and a school there. Jones was popular among the non-Natives as well as among his own people, and while the Methodists decided if he were fit to become an itinerant preacher, he continued his duties as chief of the Credit band. [74]

The Indian settlement at the Credit River had been in

existence for a year before the government knew about it and the Indians' industrious, Christian inclinations. It was only when Jones wrote on his people's behalf to request that their presents be sent to the Credit instead of wasting precious time away from their endeavours, that the government officials became curious, and went to see for themselves. Settling the Indians together had been the next idea the government planned to deploy, but the stations were to be Church of England. The Methodists were already actively pursuing this goal. They'd cleverly appointed Egerton Ryerson who had been aware of Lieutenant-Governor Sir Peregrine Maitland's plan, and had quickly established a Methodist school. It was such a success that the government accepted what they'd accomplished. But there was still hostility towards the Methodists.[75]

Jones kept his promise to Case, and in February, he came to the Bay of Quinte area: home to the *Mississauga* bands from the Kingston and Belleville area. That winter, one hundred and thirty Belleville *Mississaugas* were the first to be converted. Jones and John Crane, also from the Credit, whetted their brothers' spiritual appetites, exhorting the benefits of salvation if they'd embrace Christianity ... and left, secure in the knowledge that they'd made an impression. They'd let the seeds: the thoughts and feelings, gestate until spring when an additional forty Kingston *Mississaugas* joined their brothers from Belleville.[76]

In 1815, the first census for the area around the Bay of Quinte claimed there were two hundred and fifty-seven Indians in the area who received annuities—annual payments for lands they had surrendered. One hundred and fifty-nine of them are Bay of Quinte *Mississaugas*; ninety-eight are of the Kingston band. Twenty principal chiefs are responsible for about a dozen members each—a sharp decline from previous times when chiefs represented four or five families that in each would have an average of ten persons.[77]

By August, 1826, the Lieutenant-Governor of Upper Canada ordered, through the Indian Department, that Sacred Feathers and his Indian colleagues stop attending Methodist camp meetings. Were the "savages" getting too much religion, or did the settlers want to have exclusive love feasts? Jones was confounded "...so that if a man wants to retire to the woods to pray, who had a right to prevent him?"...but since he and his people were in the midst of building a settlement and needed the government's support, he remained silent.[78]

Shawundais

Shawundais was named for the "sultry heat" which the sun gives out in summer just before a fertilizing rain.[79] His painted face glows red like the sky at day's end. His hair is adorned with feathers; a blanket and silver ornaments hang round his neck, and mooseskins cover his legs and torso. A rifle, tomahawk and scalping knife – all drape from his tall, solid frame.[80]

Shawundais had been part of the exodus from New York State, where he was born on the banks of the Black River in 1795 or '96. He'd fought in the War of 1812, and subsequently, saw the changes in his people as they become dispossessed of land, customs and religious beliefs, to make room for settlers.

Traditional *Ojibway* religion embraced matters concerned with daily life. The Indians prayed to the *mnidoos* of those things which had sustained and nourished them; they prayed for strength and for health that would grant them a long life—in order to hunt—all integral and therefore all part of their religion. When their *mnidoos* failed them, the starvation they suffered was physical as well as spiritual.[81]

The *Ojibway* people's tradition of communication is oral. The spoken word was revered, and an orator who could hold an audience was highly respected. *Shawundais* was a popular storyteller among his own people as well as among non-Native audiences. Known for his humourous tales and 'savage' mimicry, as well as his great fund of knowledge, he kept people entertained with his wit and comical posturings.[82]

But *Shawundais* feels that the devil is in his soul, and that the Black Coat men are aware of it. They recognize the darkness there. He sees it in their eyes when they look at him. They ask him questions and he is sure they already know the answers. Even the *Anishnaabeg* preachers can see beyond the flesh of his body, to his aching heart. New thoughts churn in his mind. He sees the smiling, knowing faces of the Black Coats and feels guilty when they look at him. His people—his own children—are dying around him. But the Hats are strong; their babies have fat bellies and round apple cheeks. New sounds ring in his ears—even the birds sing with the Black Coats and the Hats. Nights that were once peaceful times to rest now stretch on forever; the silence they once brought him has become a deafening roar in his ears.

Voices beckon to *Shawundais* where he lies on a mat by the fire. He rises, blind from gazing into the flames, and follows the sound, staggering from fatigue and from the firewater that burns in his belly. Liquor helps him to forget for a while, but now his guts and head burn like a raging fire.

When his eyes adjust to the darkness, he sees torches flickering at the edges of the clearing. *Shawundais* stands alone in the shadows, beyond the gathering where he hears voices; his heart swells, pounding madly, like it wants to escape the torment in his body.

It pains and confuses *Shawundais* to watch the Hats shouting and singing. They appear happy with their *mnidoo*. But some of them look like they too have been drinking firewater: they leap in the air and roll on the ground like drunken animals. Once, just after his boys had died, he'd come upon a gathering like this one. He'd asked them for a glass of beer to help him bear his sadness, but they refused him, and kept on wailing and moaning.

Now, a Hat and his woman stand in front of the others, with Black Coats by their sides. They are shouting and waving their arms. The woman drops to the ground. She looks very drunk and they have to help her to stand. But they all appear very happy that she is drunk. *Shawundais knows* that he must belong to the devil because when he gets drunk, no one is ever happy.

A silhouette gathers shape and approaches *Shawundais*. It moves silently through the brush that has been cleared for the Black Coats' meeting. Moonlight snags a piece of silver bobbing on the advancing figure. For moments, only the cross shines in the darkness. Then a preacher appears—the cross burning from his chest. Even in the dim light of the moon, *Shawundais* can feel the eyes of the stranger penetrate him; the preacher can see through him— this man already knows the contents of his poor, tormented mind. But Shawundais must ask the question.

"They are not drunk with liquor, brother; they are drunk with religion. Come and drink the love of God with us," he is told.

On February 17th, 1826, twelve *Mississauga* men walked thirty miles to see the Indian preachers,[83] and for the next three days, the preachers, chiefs Peter Jones and John Crane, tell the *Mississaugas* of their people's accomplishments since they had become Christians. They talk about the importance of religion, and of sending their children to school. They invite the parents to send some of the *Mississauga* children back with the two chiefs, to attend school at the Credit. Some parents are of the mind that if their children live with the whites, they will lose their ability to hunt. Finally, one parent says that if his brother consents to "give up his boy", he would let his go too.[84]

Early on the morning of February 19th, *Shawundais* and others arrive at the home of settler James Howard, to buy some liquor. The settlers and the Indians all use alcohol. It softens the harsh-edged realities of their new lives together. Howard tells them about all the Indians who are going to see the Indian preachers, and offers to hitch his team to drive them. When they arrive, they can't get into the overcrowded building, and they sit—from nine in the morning until five o'clock, on a snow-covered woodpile, waiting for a chance to meet the Indian preachers. When the meeting ends, Crane and Jones invite them to attend the seven o'clock meeting. *Shawundais* is moved by one of the orations he listens to, dealing with the hereafter: a subject that had been troubling him since the death of his boys.

The two chiefs return to the Credit settlement. *Shawundais* leaves too, but has a drink with his friends before he starts on his seven-mile walk home. All the way, he continues to think about what he had heard. After four sleepless nights, he visits Brother Case. Shawundais still feels like he belongs to the devil. When he returns home Monday, he makes his first attempt at prayer:

> " I do not know how to pray—my heart is too hard—I cannot say but few words; I say this: `O Lord, I am wicked, I am wicked man, take me out from that no peace everlasting fire and dark place.' Next morning I went in the woods to pray; - no peace in my heart yet."[85]

From February until May, *Shawundais* wrestles with questions and with the confusion of giving up his Native religion for the white man's. He attends other prayer meetings. At one of them, a preacher introduces the notion of 'forgiveness' to him: a hopeful sign for *Shawundais*—though one that is later dashed at a Love Feast where the "Lord's bread" chokes him: confirmation that he belongs to the devil. He feels the sign is proven when he returns home and has no difficulty swallowing another piece of bread.

He is confused. The white man's God continues to beckon him. He returns to the woods and tries to summon his traditional religion. With a charcoal- blackened face, he fasts and prays for a vision, but his trust in the *mnidoos* has been broken, his spirit barren.[86]

Another time, *Shawundais* is in the woods with an Indian friend. *Shawundais* asks him, "Can you pray? If you can, kneel down and pray." The friend declines and defers to *Shawundais*. They both kneel, and while he tries to pray, *Shawundais* sees a vision of two floating beings. The closest tells him that he is not praying correctly; he should pray to the other being—the one who is floating further away from them—to ask for all he needs, and the closer one would negotiate for him.

Shawundais remains confused about the meaning of the vision until a devout Christian tells him that it was God's way of saying that he must pray to God the Father, in the Name of Jesus Christ, the Son.[87] The Christian also tells him that his recently deceased children had not gone to heaven because they were not baptized, that they had died pagans. This menacing thought—while he is considering Christianity—disturbs him. If this was so, he'd stay a pagan, to be with his children when he died, he thinks. A Roman Catholic woman later assures him that his children are in heaven.

In a dream, his two boys appear from a door in the sky, to stand before him. They'd traded their Indian clothing for shining white garments when they'd gone to live in their beautiful, happy home. The boys deliberate over who they are going to take there with them, finally deciding on their baby sister. When she actually dies a short time later, *Shawundais* trembles from the truth of the dream. He *knows* they are in heaven now, and wants to join them when he dies.[88] All his life, his parents had told him that "all the Indians shall go where sun sets, but the white people shall go in the *Ishpiming*".[89] At a camp meeting, he hears Peter Jones tell of the two ways: the broad way—for all manner of sinners: whites and Indians, who drank and were wicked. And the narrow way: for *all* who were good and served the Lord.[90] Brain clouded with alcohol and confusion, *Shawundais* continues to feel wicked.

That a white person would pray for a poor old Indian moved the Indians to tears; but that the Red Man would *also* be received into *Ishpiming*—by the White Man's God—was doubly powerful. "Dost thou renounce the devil and all his works?" the preacher asks a final question of the men who would be christened John Sunday, Peter Jacobs and William Beaver—all standing before him.   "Aaho," they all reply together in one loud voice.   As they say it, they lift their feet and bring them down on the floor. The chapel quakes with sound echoing through the timbers.[91] The following day, May 27th, 1826, Peter Jones, a preacher, *Shawundais* and approximately fifty Indians canoe to what the Methodists call the Hallowell Circuit, for a Quarterly meeting.

"In the afternoon we went to pray-meeting in the Old House, about five o'clock, and Peter Jones says to us, 'let us lift up our hearts to God.' I look at him; I do not understand him. I think this, if I do this—take my heart out of my body, I shall be died; however, I kneel down to pray to God. I do not know what to say to ask for religion; I only say this — 'O Keshamunedo, shahnanemeshim[92]. O Lord have mercy on me poor sinner.' By and by, the good Lord, he pour his spirit upon my poor wretched heart; then I should be happy in my heart. I feel very light; and after pray meeting, I went to tell Peter Jones how I feel in my heart: - I say to him this, ' I feel something in my heart.' Peter says to me, 'Lord bless you now.' O how glad in my heart. I look around—and look over other side a Bay—and look up—and look in the woods; the same is everything. NEW to me. I hope I got religion that day. I thank the Great Spirit what he done for me. I want to be like this which built his house upon a rock. Amen".[93]

The Nursery of Indian Missions

With the first conversion of the Mississaugas in the Bay of Quinte area on May 31,1826, a Society of Methodist Indians was organized on Grape Island: " the Insular Garden of Hesperides", a "tangled mass of vines and bushes" it was to become a Methodist landmark called the Nursery of Indian Missions.[94]

When converted, they became exhorters whose responsibility was to "awaken complacent and urge sinners and backsliders to consider their ways and repent."[95] Singing was an integral part of the Methodist doctrine, and at the Adolphustown meeting the Indians knew one hymn: "O For a Thousand Tongues to Sing My Great Redeemer's Praise," which "they sung [sic], over and over, as if always new and always good."[96]

> "O For a thousand tongues to sing
> My great Redeemer's praise!
> The glories of my God and King
> The triumphs of his grace!
> My gracious Master and my God,
> Assist me to proclaim,
> To spread through all the earth abroad
> The honours of thy name.
> Jesus!—the name that charms our fears,
> That bids our sorrows cease!
> Tis music in the sinner's ears,
> Tis life, and health and peace.
> He breaks the power of cancell'd sin,
> He sets the prisoner free;
> His blood can make the foulest clean;
> His blood avail'd for me.
> Look unto him, ye nations; own
> Your God, ye fallen race;
> Look, and be saved through faith alone,
> Be justified by grace". [97]

The Methodists' belief that the Bible was the primary standard of faith—required literate converts, and educated Indian children could be missionaries to their illiterate parents. For the first few years, the courses of study were limited to reading, writing, the study of the Bible, and learning to sing hymns.[98] The hymns of Charles Wesley spread the Methodist doctrine through the devoted students who learned as they sang.

> "...vocal music was an important and intrinsically pleasing avenue to the faculties. Teaching children moral songs would displace the ribald and frivolous amusements they had previously pursued, while turning their recreation into a means of instruction. Music, if correctly used, could refine and humanize pupils... educators claimed that since the common schools of Germany had begun to teach workers to sing, the degrading habits of intoxication so common there had been reduced."[99]

Jones' permanent settlement at the Credit was a model for settling the Indians at the Bay of Quinte, where Case leased *Zhoomin Mniss*—Grape Island—from the Indians, a formal gesture to the neighbouring settlers as well as to the *Mississaugas*. The 11-acre island is located 'in front of the township of Earnestown, County of Addington, Ontario', six miles from Belleville on Lake Ontario.[100] *Sahgeen*, a fifty-acre island, was also leased to raise cattle.

On October 16th, 1826, the *Mississaugas* signed an agreement with five men from Belleville who acted as trustees for a transaction in which the *Mississaugas* would lease their own land for five shillings for nine hundred and ninety-nine years. By making this long term commitment, the *Mississaugas* were giving the charitable community the assurance that their donations were going toward an effort that would have lasting benefits.[101] At that time, one hundred and thirty Indians had been converted and would settle there. The men from Belleville should have known that a village on eleven acres would be too small to accommodate that number of people.

When Francis Hall, clerk of the Missionary Society of the Methodist Episcopal Church in New York, visited Grape Island in 1828, he remarked that the island was too small for its intended purpose, but he tried to justify Case's decision of removing the *Mississaugas* to these islands by saying that Case had wanted to get them as far away from the white settlers' influence as possible. However, three miles from the mainland on one side of the island and five or six on the other, the island was on a thoroughfare for steamships and actually not very secluded.

In early October, 1828, the Indian children performed at the Canada Conference at Switzer's Chapel in Earnestown. At this conference, the Methodist Church in Canada became the Methodist Episcopal Church of Canada, independent from the United States. Since no bishops from across the border would be coming to future conferences, they needed a leader. Brother Case was their clear choice; after 18 years as Presiding Elder, and the conference's oldest member, he became General Superintendent. Meant only to be a temporary measure, it was a position he held for five years. He was also appointed Superintendent of Indian Missions.[102]

As early as April, 1831, the government was advising the Indians at Grape Island that they should select land on which they wanted to live so it could be surveyed. They had previously inquired about Big Island that was about two hundred acres in size. First, they were told that it had never been reserved for them—yet they'd been receiving rent of two hundred bushels of potatoes for it. Then, the government offered to survey the island for them and to remove the settlers. The *Mississaugas* were told that Big Island was already property of the Crown, but a few months later, they signed their totems on documents to legally surrender it.[103]

Despite internal problems in the Methodist Society, the island mission continued to attract publicity. A reporter for the Montreal Gazette writes in a series of articles published in the Guardian about Grape Island:

> "... the view of Grape Island, on sailing up the Bay of Quinte about sunrise, is very beautiful. The houses looming away in the distance, seem much larger and more numerous than they really are, and give the idea of a well built town. On our arrival at it, therefore, we are some thing disappointed, although calm reflection satisfies us that it is really superior to anything we had a right to expect, considering the hopeless misery in which its inhabitants were plunged a few years ago, before the indefatigable labours of the Missionaries were the means, under God of contributing to exalt them to their present comparatively respectable condition".[104]

Sylvester Hurlburt, a teacher at Grape Island pens a report, also published in the series:

> " ...perhaps the female school was never doing better. The girls love and respect their female teacher, and are improving well. Most of the men are busily employed in gathering their crops. The Indians certainly feel the advantage of industry, and manifest an increasing desire to improve their temporal circumstances.—We have to regret that some of the Indians about Gananoque and Kingston, who have occasionally resorted to the island, have been led into intemperate habits, so that the Society has lost, by expulsion, ten of its members. This is to be attributed to their wandering state; much difficulty has been felt in leading a portion of this body to a fixed residence, as certain white men have taken much pains to make them dissatisfied with their religious friends at the island, as well as to induce them to return to their former habits of drinking. The result is that they are fast relapsing into their former dissipation and misery ".[105]

NEW BEGINNINGS : *Zhoomín Mníss*

A young woman sits at a makeshift desk, grasping a pencil stub in her fist. She moves the pencil across the page in slow, deliberate motions. A snake-like mark slithers down the page. Beside it she draws an apple with a long stem, then a short stick with half an upside down curl coming out of it. Another apple, then a long stick with a curl from its middle right down to the line where the big stick started. She has learned that separately, each character can be spoken, and each one has its own sound. Sounded together they make words, like the new name the Black Coats have given her: Sarah.

She still dreams—sometimes when her eyes are open—about Medicine Woman, who had given her the name *Ishpiniibin*. Sometimes she doesn't recognize her new name when it is called. The letters don't mean anything to her. They don't fit. She'd like a name that started with butterflies instead of snakes. Like Betsy.

Her uncle has a new name too, though some people still call him *Shawundais*. His English name is John Sunday, like the first day of the week. He doesn't drink firewater any more. He and other Indian men here are helping the preachers in their work for the Great Spirit.

Sarah and her people became Christians in blossom time, when the *Anishnaabeg* preachers visited. It was a time when the air was sweet and humming with new life. It was a time of hope. Now that they have been baptized, her people will go to *Ishpiming* with the white people when they die. Sarah remembers the smiling faces that leaned into her streaming face the day she became a Christian, water dripping down her face, mixing with her tears. Before the preachers left that day, William Beaver—the first of her people to be converted, and Uncle John, are appointed to be class leaders. They would be responsible for watching over the Indians on Grape Island, to see that they keep praying like they'd been taught, to see that they are working hard, that they aren't drinking firewater, and that they are living in peace. The two men were to assure the Indians that, if they did all of these things, they would be Christians and live well. [106] Uncle John and William Beaver would see to it.

In the middle of June, fifty-eight of her people go to a camp meeting in the place they call Adolphustown. The preachers say her people are "Christian Indians" and that they should go. It is at the place of the springs where they all share the sweet, clean water. The camp has two entrances and there are Hats standing at each. They keep out people who are drunk or people who could make trouble. Before the meeting ends, the keepers of the gates say that three or four thousand people are inside.

Pine torches light every part of the clearing —even in the gully near the fence where Sarah and her people are sent. There are many Hats there. She hears them talking about her people, that the Indians acted "orderly" and "prepared" when they arrived, setting up camp before they cooked a meal.

Many of the *Mississaugas* are baptized at that love feast. The Indians' tears flow like the water used to bless them. White people pray for them. Some of the Indians fall down and have to be carried back to their campsite. [107]

Blossom time has passed and the fruit is ripe from the nourishment of the passing seasons. The air is sweet, though the winds blow cool messages of winter's approach. Many Indians are Christians now. It is like a fever running through the people; everyone is catching it. Her people say this is a good fever.

In July, Uncle John and John Moses travel north to Lake Simcoe with Peter Jones where he prays with Indians there and reads to them from the Bible. Uncle John and Moses are called Exhorters. Their work is to tell stories about how they'd come along the path and found the Great Spirit. How twisted the path had been, how rigourous the journey. They warn of a terrible future if the Indians don't accept the Great Spirit into their lives. They talk about schools for Indian children. [108] Indians can have everything if they become Christians.

It is October and Sarah and her people call Grape Island their home. She remembers coming here with her mother in late summer while the men fished, when they picked the dark blue fruit that hung heavy on the vines, never thinking that one day they might live every season here. She silently shapes the forbidden word with her lips: *Zhoomin Mniss*, the island's Indian name. Her people say that their old ways are bad and they suffer because of it. They must never speak Indian. They need to live in one place, like the Hats who build fences. Her mind drifts to memories of running like a fawn over an open meadow where strawberries grew. She draws a field and dots it with tiny plants and berries. A deer. A tree, and birds. She prints their names beside each plant and animal. Children must learn to read and write; she recites another rule in her mind. She likes to read. They all must worship God inside the walls of a church, Sarah continues the litany. She doesn't know why, when she first prayed in a field.

Some of the men go to Belleville where five Hats say they will let the *Mississaugas* live on Grape Island. It is *already* their island, but the five men say they will be the trustees of the land now, and that the *Mississaugas* need to pay rent for the land. They draw their totems on a piece of paper called a lease. They rent another island, Sahgeen, where they will raise cattle.[109]

The Black Coat Man, Father Case, is very happy to help them, but he and his church have no money to buy equipment and supplies that the *Mississaugas* need to live on the island—in houses like white people. Some of the Hats give the church money because they want to see Sarah's people settled on the island, staying in one place, learning to be Christian farmers. They have been sent six hoes from the church, and even the young children have been taught to use them.[110] Trees have been cut down and the earth has been turned over in fields. Seeds are buried in long lines under the earth. Sarah has never lived with so many people—there are 130—on such little land. The *wiigwaaman* stand very close together. The preacher comes across the water from Belleville to pray with them when he can.

After the ice thaws in the spring, the men cut logs on the *Tyendinaga* settlement, near the Moira River. The logs are floated out to a sawmill where once they are cut into lumber, are tied into rafts and steered back to the island for use in construction.[111]

The *Anishnaabeg* preacher will come in Blossom time again this next year, to stay on the island with the *Mississaugas*. When his canoe is first seen approaching, Sarah and many others run down to the shore to meet him. They weep to see the Indian preacher, who had changed their lives, among them once again. Some of them collapse there, so full are their hearts.

Now he will help them build their houses. He went out fishing with Reverend Atwood and caught fifty catfish. He prays with them.[112] They sing together now. They are learning hymns and stories from the Bible. When they don't understand, William

Beaver tells them in Indian, meanings of words in the Bible. He has them say the words over and over again until they know them in their hearts.[113]

The Methodist people call the island the Nursery of Indian Missions and from it sixteen Indians will become missionaries. They will go from Grape Island to far away places to take the Great Spirit's word to other Indian people. Many visitors come to see them.[114] Some give money, others gifts, when they see that the Indians are becoming just like white people. One day, a team of oxen arrives on a barge; later, three cows bellow across the water on a steamship that is also carrying tools and supplies for them.

But Sarah is confused. Many of the settlers do not read or write. They drink firewater—it is said you aren't a heavy drinker unless you drink more than four glasses a day.[115] The Indians were learning to be like perfect white people, but many of the white people were acting like bad Indians. She remembers what Jacob Peter had said at a meeting.

"White people have been Christians for a long time, but still they get drunk; they still tell lies and do bad things on the day of the Great Spirit, the Sabbath." Then he pointed to the Indians. "They don't know the words to pray. They don't know how to read. But since the Great Spirit came to them, they have been good Christians."[116]

A shaft of early evening's light slants through the window, glancing Sarah's raven hair. She closes her eyes, and lets the ray of energy play on the roofs of her eyelids. They come into this building now to learn from their teacher, Richard Phelps. In the evenings, it is where they come for prayer meetings. They used to see Brother Phelps kneeling on a mat when his sleeping place was at the back of the building.

They just buried John Moses. Many other Indian people died this year too. Before the ice was thick on the lake, a Black Coat named Solomon Waldron arrived; he and Mr. Phelps are both staying with them on Grape Island now. They say the Indians are sick and dying from all the Shkiniwaqboo they drank before accepting the Great Spirit into their lives.

The channel churns with passing steamships. Hats visit the island—women in long, fancy cloth dresses, men with tall black hats. Envelopes are slipped into Father Solomon's hand as he walks with them to the shore.[117] Sarah wears cloth dresses now and is learning to read. If she could read better, Father

Solomon would show her the papers where it talked about her people and their village in the "picturesque Bay of Quinte" where "Christian industry among the Native people thrives"...where they are building a church, a school, and a hospital. Visitors write about some of the work they witness: scenes of men whittling axe handles, smoothing broom handles; women were churning butter or packing freshly made cheese into new baskets of their own crafting.

Another story describes the church bell ringing as the steamboats passed, and young melodic voices drifting across the water to the passengers leaning on the rails of the passing ships. She could have added that beyond the passengers' view, Father Solomon's arms were flailing about behind the bushes, as he directed Sarah and the rest of the young people to begin singing when the steamship passed. She watches some of the Hats leaning on the railings with pencils and paper like she used in the school. They look at the island and the Indians, then they look down at the paper and write words, or make pictures. Even if Sarah could read, she wouldn't know that writers like Anna Jameson, Susanna Moodie and her sister Catharine Parr Traill, or artists like Paul Kane were on those steamboats, sketching and jotting notes.

Mister Phelps is teaching them about taking care of animals, about growing crops. The women paddle or snowshoe—depending on the season, two miles, twice a day, to milk the cows on Sahgeen Island. Then, they travel another mile and a half to Huff's Island, to get firewood. The lake is a misty looking-glass at dawn, a rosy blush at sunset when their paddles silently slice the water.

Sarah knows numbers and measurements now. It is winter and they have built ten log houses that are eighteen feet wide and twenty feet long. They say eight of them will be ready for the Indians to live in this winter. Trees are cut into logs, then sawed into flat pieces called shingles. The men will need many of them to cover the roofs of ten houses. Smoke from the fires in these houses exits up chimneys, and all of these are made from square stones the colour of earth. Some families won't have to sleep in their *wiigwaaman* this winter, and Mister Phelps has his own house now too.[118]

Some of the men have gone hunting and won't be here this fall. That is another confusing issue: the Black Coats say that hunting is not good in the eyes of the Great Spirit—that her people are supposed to be farmers, and to raise animals for meat. But the Black Coats act like they don't see the deer and fish that cover the bottoms of the canoes when the men return from hunting. The meat always finds its way to the dinner table, and the Black Coats always appear to enjoy what's set before them.

Some Hats say that the Black Coats are protecting the Indians, keeping them away from the Hats who would feed the Indians liquor, then abuse them. Now the Hats can't reach the Indians, so they make up stories about the preachers, like, when Father Solomon and his new bride were living on Grape Island. His wife got sick and left the island to stay with her brother on the mainland where there were doctors. Father Solomon preached at Belleville too, and he was often tired from paddling across the water or from walking on the ice back and forth from the island, so he would spend the night in Belleville. The explanation of their actions was that the couple had parted because he had been "guilty with an Indian female."[119]

Peter Jones and Father Case come to visit in early January. Forty children are with their teacher, Miss Yeomans. The men trudge around the island through the drifting snow. They act excited when they see freshly finished axe handles, shovels, ladles, trays and brooms neatly stacked against the houses. By the middle of the harsh snow that month, there are 172 living on Grape Island, including the Kingston band. They have been put into six classes all with Indian teachers.[120]

Uncle John isn't with them on the island—the Black Coats keep sending him on trips to talk to white people about what has happened to him, how he is different now that he has found the Great Spirit. At blossom time, Uncle John comes back from talking trips to New York and Philadelphia. Father Case and Peter Jacobs are with him. Sarah hears how her uncle had spoken to the Hats in *Ojibway*, of how they'd cried even though they didn't understand what he said. He talked and the Hats gave him gifts. From them, twenty families receive bundles of enough ticking to cover their straw beds.[121]

Two women accompany the men back to Grape Island. One is called Hester Ann Hubbard. Hetty is another name her close friends call her. She is a shy woman who will be a teacher here. The other woman is Eliza Barnes, a preacher, like the men.[122]

It is 1828. The Grape Island gardens are full of vegetables, and the women are busy making baskets. Before Peter Jones arrived, the *Mississaugas* counted up 100 baskets of every size and shape, to show him. This time they could also offer him maple sugar.

When a camp meeting was held near a place called Haldimand in June, the Grape Island Indians went. The Indian children were part of the meeting, where they sang hymns and recited parts of the Ten Commandments in English. The Hats smiled at the little brown-skinned children, and at the end of the meeting put money on the plate that was passed around.[123]

Two or three white men called mechanics come to help construct the buildings on Grape Island, but after a while they leave when there is no money to pay them. By the end of summer, twenty-seven log buildings stand on the island—seven can be lived in. The mechanics had taught the Indians how to cut and place the logs, how to make shingles and put them on, how to make furniture.

They pray in a chapel now. The women and girls have a schoolhouse, and there is a log building at one end of the island where the women go at the time of their moons, and to have their babies. It is called a hospital.

Two bulky shapes form a distance from the shore in the early morning fog and as they draw closer, two women are seen straddling two logs lashed together, their makeshift-raft bobbing like a stick in the rolling waves. They've come from the mainland four miles away, paddling with pieces of boards. It wasn't the first time Indians from the other shore had tried to get here.

Sarah wraps one of the treaty blankets around her shoulders as the canoe glides through the still September evening. The Grape Island Indians have been to Belleville. They return now with gifts from Indian Agent Clench. She sorts through the piles stacked on the bottom of the canoe. He'd given each of them two blankets and enough cloth to make coats. The men each receive a pair of trousers, two shirts, guns and ammunition. Back on the island, they'll divide up the kettles, pots and pans for each house.[124]

Waapoone—butterflies—darken the skies, drifting on the northern breeze. Sarah kneels by a cache of freshly-dug potatoes. She brushes loose soil from each one, and drops them in the bushel beside her. This is the last basket, and when it is filled there'll be 300 bushels of potatoes for the winter. Her gaze drifts skyward to the lilting orange and black specks, memories of summer wafting southward with them.

In October, at a missionary meeting in Belleville where Father Case is preaching, Miss Hubbard leads the children in singing hymns and speaking by heart from the Bible for the white people. One of the *Mississauga* boys, eight-year-old Allan Salt, thanks them for supporting Grape Island. His father and mother had begun to pray two years ago, he tells them. His mother is dead now, but she had prayed right up to her death. His father had sent him to school at Grape Island, where he and sixty other children were learning to read the Good Book.

Allan Salt tells them that in the *wiigwaam* it had been cold, his people hungry. Now they have plenty to eat, and live in good houses like their white friends in Belleville who had helped them. He prays to *Gzhe-mnidoo* to reward them for their kindness.[125]

In February, 1829, Miss Barnes and Peter Jones come to the island and leave with Father Case and his bride-to-be, Miss Hubbard, on a trip to raise funds for the Indian Missions. They take Indian children with them and tour until mid-May. The fields are ready for planting by the time they return, and when they arrive, the Indians learn that Father Case and Miss Hubbard were married while they were in a place called New York City.[126]

By late summer, Grape Island has fifty-six students at the two schools. There are twenty-five Belleville *Mississauga* families of one hundred and sixteen members; and twenty Kingston *Mississauga* families with ninety-two members.[127] Peter Jones returns in September, and again for two weeks in October. Trades are taught to the Indians in a 'workhouse' or 'vocational school'. By fall, twenty-six buildings are completed, crops are growing on fifty acres, and twenty thousand feet of lumber has been cut.[128]

It is 1830. *Mississaugas* from Grape Island leave to go on talking trips with the Black Coats. In March, John Simpson travels with the missionary John Benham, to help set up a school and mission at *Sah-kung* on Lake Huron.[129] At the end of July, John Sunday and John Paul travel by themselves from the Credit Mission to Penetanguishene and the Mackinaw by way of Detroit. It is like old times for them, walking over the countryside, canoeing, fishing. They sleep under the stars most evenings, in barns when they can find them. Mother Earth once again provides for them when the men need to fill their bellies.

They spread the Creator's Word to all who will listen. Father Case says they are perfect travelling preachers: they don't need to pack much. They can build canoes and hunt with bows and arrows. They know which plants are edible, which are medicines. They are comfortable on both land and water. The Indian people they meet are happy to see Uncle John and John Paul.

In Detroit, they say that some of the Indians there threw away all their rattles and *wampum* bags when they accepted Christianity. The two men don't reach home until early October—not yet winter, but with threadbare clothes and worn-out shoes, they are chilled to the bone, and Uncle John's pleurisy attacks have worsened.[130]

Peter Jones appears in late summer and spends a month on Grape Island. He hears the first cries of Eliza Jane Case, born on the 10th day of August. He also becomes a real minister this summer. A blacksmith lives there with them now, along with Mr. & Mrs. Case. There are one hundred and twenty-five Indian students and two teachers for the schools.[131]

The lake has started to boil like soup in a cauldron and high winds and storms constantly pound the island. The waters are so rough that one of the men couldn't get back when he went out on the bay in a canoe. A steamship drew up close to the man, and some of the crew and passengers saw him. They fished him out of the water and managed to revive him. When he returns to the island, the smell of liquor is strong on his breath. He explains that the captain of the steamship had made him drink a glass of whiskey to warm himself. It is the first time in years that even the smell of liquor had been on Grape Island. It upset everyone and for a day, the chastened man is the centre of their attention. One by one, each adult talks to him about the Great Spirit's way; then, someone else prays for him, and they all make him promise that he will never drink whiskey again.[132]

In their homes, fathers lead their families in prayer three times a day. On Sundays, they begin to pray together at six o'clock in the morning. Later, there is Sunday school, then a church service at eleven o'clock. At two o'clock, there is a session they call a Meeting of Inquiry. Then there are class meetings at four o'clock, and a prayer meeting at seven o'clock. They are lucky to sit down between the chores of farming, before it is time for praying.

There are twenty-nine buildings now: twenty-three houses, a chapel, a schoolhouse, a hospital, a general storehouse, a blacksmith shop and a mechanics shop. James Crawford and

William Salt have become good carpenters and the Mohawks have hired them to help build a meeting house at their settlement. The money the two men earn goes to the Grape Island Mission.[133]

Sarah wakes to the noise of a rasping saw and the tap-tap-tapping of hammers. It is almost light, but she recognizes the noises that had been with her in dreamtime. The men are building little wooden boxes to put the young ones in who have passed on. Their graves will be marked with two pieces of wood tied in crosses. These children will go to *Ishpiming* now. Their markers are starting to fill in a corner of the cemetery. The new people who come to live on the island bring sickness with them. Sounds of sadness, wailing and whimpering can be heard from every part of the island. Sarah hears them from the hospital where she bathes the children's hot spotted bodies with cool water. Their helpless little sobs tug on her heart; their coughs sound like a pack of barking dogs. This year, seventeen will die from diseases called measles and whooping cough.[134]

The Indians miss Father Case. They won't see their *Anishnaabeg* preacher, Peter Jones, either. He's gone across the Salt Water to England. It is a time of many losses. Among them is Brother John Paul, Uncle John's exhorter. Mrs. Case has been sick since before Eliza Jane was born. She suffered for seven months from a sadness in her heart. By the middle of September, a box is being made for her. In her dying hours, she holds her six-month-old daughter, Eliza Jane; the blanket swaddling the baby are damp with tears. A woman stands beside the bed. She is Brother Hurlburt's wife, and will become mother to Eliza Jane, given to her in trust when Mrs. Case dies.[135]

In 1828, Sarah and her people had travelled to Belleville to get their annual presents from the Indian agent, but in 1831, they are meant to go to Kingston—some sixty miles away. It is harvest time and they can't afford that much time away. The Black Coats ask, on their behalf, that the presents be delivered to Grape Island.[136]

John Simpson came home from mission work at *Sahgeeng*. He spent a lot of time with the Black Coats, talking, listening, and praying. At a love feast, he'd told a story about himself, of how wicked he'd been before he found religion. Of how troubled he'd been. He thanked Uncle John who'd kept telling him—over and over—about Jesus. Uncle John had prayed to the Great Spirit for John Simpson because Uncle John understood the man's trouble; he'd wrestled with the same torments.

John Simpson told of how he'd gone to a camp meeting, and prayed for a blessing on himself, a poor Indian. Before he left that camp meeting he said his heart felt very light, that he felt blessed all over—his soul and his body too. When that happened his heart changed, and he was able to love everybody.[137] Sarah enjoys hearing him talk. His words are a comfort. He is good for the people, but after three months, he will leave again.

A young man appears at the door of John Sunday's house. He asks for her uncle and Sarah invites him inside. She has never seen him before, yet she feels comfortable in his presence, like he is family. He has brought smoked fish for her uncle and a message from his parents. His name is Joshua Moses and he will live here and go to school. He speaks English a little, but very slowly. Sarah's aunt stirs meat in a pan on the stove; Sarah chops vegetables, straining to hear what the two men are talking about. Chairs scrape, throats clear, logs crackle and she hears nothing but low tones and the odd hearty laugh from across the room. When Joshua Moses leaves, Uncle John crosses the room and stands between his wife and niece.

"He's a fine young man, Sarah. He'd make a good husband for you by and by." That was all Uncle John said, but she knew the reason for the visit. His parents had decided it was time for their son to marry, and had sent Joshua to Grape Island with John Simpson, to come to school, and to take a wife.

Sarah Moses. Missus Sarah Moses. Missus Joshua Moses. Mister and Missus Joshua Moses. At night, she practises writing her name in a notebook she keeps by her bed. She will share her bed and his name. A short time later, early breezes from the south carry the fragrance of grape and cherry blossoms up the aisle to the altar where Uncle John stands before Joshua and Sarah. Before all of their Grape Island brothers and sisters, the couple vows to love, honour and obey each other unto death.

In June, Uncle John climbs into a canoe with two other men to go on missionary work, like the Black Coats. They will visit the northwestern tribes near the Mackinaw and Sault Ste. Marie.[138] Uncle John will be paid twelve pounds, ten shillings, for half a year's work as a missionary. He will attend school the other half, on Grape Island.[139]

But when her uncle and the other men go away, their families don't have any money. The Black Coats must borrow money until they are able to get some help from across the Salt Water.

It is in the middle of winter when men from Grape Island snowshoe to the shore of the mainland and get on a train headed west, to attend the Grand Council meeting at the Credit where they will ask for titles to their lands, and for more land—a township—to be provided for them, to serve as a place new people could go to instead of the already bulging Grape Island. Many Indians are following the way of the Black Coats. At present, they say there are twelve hundred converted Indians in the Methodist Society, and two thousand in the Indian schools. [140]

In early August, there is a conference where many decisions are made. Uncle John advances from being an exhorter to a missionary—they call it "on trial"—until he becomes fully-fledged. He'll be posted to *Kawawenah* Bay, near Sault Ste.Marie, on the south shore of Lake Superior, for seven months. [141] Father Case is appointed to be the missionary on Grape Island.

After the conference, Peter Jones returns to the island with Father Case. This is the year a disease called cholera will kill many white people as well as Indians, and while Jones is visiting, he gets very sick. The population of the island is now only one hundred and eight, but even though the numbers have dropped, they are still overcrowded. By the following year there will be only eighty-one Indians left.

Father Case still believes in what he is doing, though people are dying around him. He says they have made great progress on the island. When they first came here they were starving, shoeless and in rags. Now they have clothing and food and they follow the Great Spirit's way. [142]

Father Case continues to travel a lot of the time. Their teacher, Sylvester Hurlburt, has written to him about their hardships and their need for land. James Crawford has rented twenty acres from a white farmer for them; they're also using Goose Island, a field on Huff's and another island at the head of the bay. Mr. Hurlburt tells Father Case that they are trying their hardest to make ends meet.

But he didn't tell him that many of Sarah's people are adrift without their Black Coat leaders, and that many are leaving the island for Kingston. There is no missionary on Grape Island to guide them and only visits by the Belleville preacher when he is able to come. Mr. Hurlburt, who works at the boys' school, is like a missionary, but preaching isn't his job, and Sarah and her people miss the teachings of the Black Coats. Sarah hears that Kingston is a bad place for the *Mississaugas*. When they go there the white people give them liquor and try to turn them against the Black Coats and their friends on the Island.[143]

On the 28th of August, 1833, Father Case marries his second wife, Eliza Barnes, in the face of a country suffering economic depression and a cholera epidemic. Grape Island has only forty-eight children in the schools. The following year, Uncle John is appointed missionary to Grape Island, but he doesn't stay there very much either.[144]

At a Quarterly Meeting held on the island, the *Mississaugas* give forty pounds to the Missionary Society, and surrender Grape Island.[145]

Uncle John speaks in English:

> *"Dear Brothers, it is now little better than eleven years since I first began to serve the Lord. Sometimes I find it very hard to get along— sometimes it just like when I was in a swamp surrounded by flies, I had to make a fire and smoke them away; so in religion I have to make a good fire in my heart to keep away wicked thoughts and bad spirits. I am very happy today, and hope to get to heaven by and by."*[146]

ALDER[S]VILLE: The Mecca of Indian Missions

The first families abandon their island home when the snows of 1835 are still deep. Sleighs follow the broken trail across the lake to the mainland like a jingling train gliding along on silver ribbons. It is March and winter will soon be gone, yet blankets of snow continue to cover them in layers. They cut north at Trenton, and follow trails where the horses wouldn't sink into the snow.

But some of the Indians who leave then won't live to see their new home in Alder[s]ville. Those who travel by canoe in May have an easier time, though the big lake frothed and seethed with whitecaps. Others follow the Trent River. Sarah and her family canoe along the north shore of Lake Ontario, to Cobourg. The fishing is good, the journey an old memory. They camp one night on the shores south of Grafton. In the morning, the women pack away their camp, while the grandmothers keep the fires going; the men are out fishing, and soon they will eat. One man stands on the bow of a canoe. He's seen sturgeons and is getting ready to spear one. He balances, a foot on each gunnel, but slipped and lost his footing just as he raised his spear to throw it into the water. They hear the splash as he tumbles in after it.[147]

It is a long journey from Grape Island; the exodus continues over the course of the next two years, until all have left the island by spring 1837.[148] At Cobourg, the men carry the canoes, the women and children follow with the possessions that they'd been able to stow. The portage from the shore of Lake Ontario to Rice Lake begins with a steady climb. Their bodies lean in the direction they are headed, bent with the weight of their belongings. When they can see the next body of water over the rolling hills below them, they call to others further back, reassuring them that the worst is over.[149] They are almost home. In the lowlands, mosquitoes and black flies have swarmed around the children, leaving them in welts and whimpering. They follow the shoreline of Rice Lake eastward until they have to portage again, before getting to their new home called

Alder[s]ville, a village in the township of Alnwick. The Black Coats would call it the Mecca of Indian Missions.[150]

Sarah stands among her people, looking at a piece of paper. There are squares on the paper and the Black Coat says each one is a fifty-acre lot. There are three thousand, four hundred and four acres. The lots look neat on the crisp white page, but outside, the land they look at is forest. Sarah's people have been told that some of the trees from this place have been cut down to be used for the masts of tall ships, like the one that carries Peter Jones across the Salt Water. Many trees will have to be cut down before they can live in houses like they had on Grape Island. The men think about the houses they'd built and left behind, of all the work that had to be done here. After years of living in houses and sleeping on beds, they were back in *wiigwaaman* in the wilderness once again. Children died. Two families have stayed on the island to farm the land and harvest crops. Sarah's people and their animals would have starved that year if it weren't for the six hundred bushels of seed crops from Grape Island.

Uncle John is a preacher now, but his health is poor and he must take care of himself. Sarah thinks about the teas Medicine Woman made for people when they were sick. She could take care of him here if he stayed on the island, but the Black Coat man who lives across the Salt Water is taking Uncle John home with him. Uncle John will dress in Indian clothes and talk to the Hats at their churches. He will make money for his relations at home, the year he is away, but he will worry about them and the other tribes who are suffering.[151]

Uncle John writes to the Black Coats from England that winter. He is concerned about the Indians who'd been taken from their villages and made to live on a rock of an island where nothing can grow. The people will die.[152] Why does the Great Father allow the Indian people to be moved around when they are trying to be like white people? They'd built schools and churches, they lived in houses—not *wiigwaaman*—yet they were made to move. His people needed to feel certain about their future.

When he returns from England, he talks to his people. He stands at the front of the meeting room. There is a sparkle in his eyes again, and when speaks to his people, the room grows quiet as the night. It is crowded; many people stand, some lean against the walls and others sit on window sills. The children are at the front on the floor. Sarah stands, jiggling a child straddled on her hip. Her uncle looks stronger now.

He tells them stories about his travels across the Salt Water, about the meetings he had with rich people. She can't understand why the white people wanted to see him dressed like an Indian, when white people here wanted Indians to be like white people.

Chuckles and snorts ripple through the room as Uncle John tells them about the time he talked to the people in a place called Plymouth. Those people had been disappointed because he was dressed like they were, so he mimed for them, his face contorted, hands snaking over his head, to show them how he used to look, with a face covered in red paint and feathers stuck in his hair. He didn't wear it any more because the Bible said he is a new creature and the Ten Commandments were his new tomahawk.[153]

He had a message from the Black Coats, something he must tell all Indians. He begins with his own people:

> *"Brothers, - A great deal of land and great deal of water is between us. You have never seen us, and we do not know your faces; but you and we pray to the same Great Spirit who made the red men and the white men. We are Brothers.*

> *Brothers, - You have given up a great deal of land to the chiefs of the white men. We are sorry to hear it. The chiefs of the white men try to persuade you to go farther back in the woods. We are sorry to hear it. For times to come we will tell you what you must do.*

> *You must never drink fire-water. The white man gives fire-water to make your brains like dung; he then laughs at you, and you go further back in the wood.*

> *Brothers, - You must learn to get dollars. To get dollars, rear sheep and pigs, cows and horses, turkeys and geese.*

Brothers, - At the end of every six moons take some of the animals to the towns of the white men, to sell them for dollars.

Brothers, - Lay up corn and dried grass for yourselves and for your animals during winter; if you have more than you want, sell some of your corn to the white men, your neighbours.

Brothers, - Cultivate your good land, sow potatoes and corn, beet and rye, oats and onions. Oats are very good when ground into meal. Onions are very good when cooked with meat and with deer's meat.

Brothers, - Cut down good trees, and saw them into planks; send the planks to the town and sell them for dollars.

Brothers, - Buy with the dollars, blankets and kettles of iron, cotton shirts and cotton for the squaws— buy spades and round knives to cut the corn—buy axes and hand-saws—buy light ploughs made of iron.

Brothers, - Do not sell any more land. Tell your children not to sell any more land. If the Governor says, "give me some of your land," say to him, "No, we have cleared off trees, we work at it, we sow seed, we will not leave it, we will not go farther back in the woods."

Do not speak words which cut to the Governor; speak to him words of "sugar", make him your friend.

Brothers, - Try to get title-deeds from the Governor— title-deeds for the land where you live now. Go to the Governor and say to him, "We have cleared the land from trees, we have sowed, and we have cut corn, we have built houses and barns: give us a title-deed for our land." If the Governor does not give the title-deed the first time, go to him again, and again, and again, until you get the title-deed. The writing must be registered in the council-house for writing. Keep the title-deed in your church: show it to your sons and daughters. May the Great Spirit keep fire away from his house.

Brothers, - We are glad to hear that many red men can read the great word, and that they love the Great Spirit who sends it. It is sent to the red man and the white man. We are glad to know that you have missionaries and schools in some of your towns.

Brothers, - Settle in little towns. Attend to the Great Word which the missionaries read to you.

Brothers, - Send your little ones to school. Come out of the wiigwaam and out of the darkness, and dwell in the light.

Brothers, - May the Great Spirit teach you to know and to love the great word. May you receive it into your hearts. [154]

Gardens and Orchards: Manual Labour Schools

Northumberland County was slower to populate than lands to the south. Land to the north was still considered Indian territory, and would-be settlers chose other areas out of fear that the Indians who had surrendered the land in 1818 under the Gunshot Treaty of 1787 would get their revenge.[155]

Still, in the early 1800s, the county was alive with plans for development. In 1820, the Trent Canal was proposed, and after being shelved once, was revived again in the 1830s. In 1831, one of the first railway projects in Upper Canada was in the works to connect Cobourg to Peterborough. In 1835, a survey crew charted one hundred and ten miles, from Rice Lake to Lake Simcoe.[156] By 1854, the Rice Lake Plank Road connected Cobourg to Harwood, and when the Rice Lake Bridge was finished and in operation from the "Indian Village"—Hiawatha— the north shore of the lake connected with Cobourg. However, the three-mile trestle was not braced properly and couldn't stand up to the severity of winter.

Drunkeness was the vice and curse of the country; barnburning, murder, and robbery were common occurrences. "Old Sorrel" was a common punishment of the day: when the guilty person was painted with tar, covered with feathers, tied to a rail and dragged behind a horse.[157]

Alderville is intersected by a highway and borders the crossroads village of Roseneath, that in the 19th century, boasted every kind of establishment from hotels to undertakers and milliners. The boundaries of Alderville are the north part of 1st Concession and the south part of the 2nd Concession of Alnwick Township for one and a half miles.

Methodist reports make Alderville sound like a prosperous, manicured village with orchards and gardens, complete with church and steeple, but by September, 1837, only fifty acres had been cleared. However, their gardens are full of vegetables and it is predicted that the new village will be completed before winter. Each house is to have a garden in front and an orchard in the back.[158] But thankfully, families continue to farm on Grape

Island where gardens and fields are already established.

The government continued to change policies regarding Indians, from settling them all on Manitoulin Island, where they'd eventually become extinct, to a return to gradual assimilation through schooling. The government told the Indians that they would be given deeds to their remaining land; however, by 1840, nothing had been done. When the split occurred that year between the British and Canadian Wesleyan Methodists, Alderville remained in the British camp because of John Sunday's fondness for the country that had recently treated him so well. [159]

Partial funding was approved for twelve out of seventeen boarders, and by 1845, thirty children were enrolled at the Alderville school. Case persuaded the Indians to give one hundred pounds of their annuity toward its operation.

The following year at a General Council of the Chiefs and Principal men held at Orillia, the leaders were further persuaded to give one quarter of their annuities for twenty-five years towards manual labour schools. Case reasoned that this investment would provide their children with a superior level of education. Education would enable them to be doctors and lawyers. They'd already seen their warriors become preachers.

Case reasoned, but the government was not so subtle. The Indians were told that for years the government had been spending all kinds of money trying to elevate them to a level equal to the white man, but because of their "unsettled and wandering habits", the efforts had been fruitless. Therefore, they are to abandon their detached villages and live in large settlements.

Manual labour schools would be established on eternally secure land—for which they would give one quarter of their annuities towards the education of their children. They are to give up their "hunting and roving" and to become farmers...or else the government would not approve expenditures for provisions. They are also to build their own houses instead of paying white people to do it for them. They are told that they don't know the value of education nor how to govern themselves. Their children shall be "sent to schools where they will *forget* their Indian habits, and be instructed in all the necessary arts of civilized life, and become one with their white brethren. In these schools they will be well taken care of, be comfortably dressed, kept clean and given plenty to eat. The adults will not be forced from their present locations. They may remove or remain, as they please, but their children must go." They are given an ultimatum: "it may be the last time you will have so good an offer [and if you don't comply] disgrace will attach to your character".[159a]

Three locations for the schools were proposed: Owen Sound, Munceytown and Alderville. John Sunday and the Chief Waubatik from Owen Sound agreed to sign and give money—but weren't going to move anywhere. The others—all but Mud Lake, Scugog, Lake Huron and Lake Simcoe—also agreed to provide funds for the schools, but they weren't willing to move either. The dissenters did not send their children—or provide funds—until 1849.[160]

Manual labour schools were costlier to run than other schools, and the Methodists were reluctant to open them without the government's support because, once opened, the Indian Department and Anderson would have the Methodists under their collective thumb. Conditions were imposed on the schools, and a triangle of control began—or continued—in a different form. When money came from the other previously dissenting reserves, a two-storey brick building was built in 1849, with a two hundred-acre farm attached, of which only sixteen acres had been cleared. The Alderville school would serve the north-east part of the province, Mount Elgin the south-west.[161]

While in England, John Sunday was in the company of Rev. Robert Alder, Secretary of the Missionary Society of the Welseyan Church in England—after whom Alder[s]ville was named. Sunday was accompanied to an interview with Lord Glenelg, to establish formal recognition that the Indians were the original proprietors of the land, and to be assured that since they had become Christians, and had built schools and churches, that they wouldn't be removed from their lands, as the government had recommended. Editorials appearing in British newspapers claimed that sending the Indians to the wilderness would " protect them from the evils of semi-civilization."

But the government held firm despite pressure from the Methodists.

> 'The Methodist Ministers might just as well declare, that when wild Beasts roar at each other it is to complain of the Want among them of Marriage Licences, for Animals understand these "Documents" just as well as Indians understand Title Deeds."[162]

When the government declared the day school plan a failure, the Methodists agreed that few of their charges had been adequately Europeanized. Government then approved the idea of manual labour schools, but no financing for them.[163] Peter Jones realized from his ten years at the Credit Mission, that the children needed to be away from the influence of their parents if they were to develop new habits.[164]

Case, who was virtually retired from the politics of the Methodist Movement, took on the project of establishing a manual labour school—on a small scale—initially for young women to be taught home economics: spinning, knitting, butter and cheese processing. Sales from dairy products were intended to support the institution.[165] The manual labour school opened its doors in 1839; in 1848, it evolved into an industrial school to serve the Indians of Lake Huron, Simcoe, Saugeen and Owen Sound, and the Mississaugas of Alnwick, and those of Rice, Mud and Scugog lakes, "all of which bands contributed from their funds for the maintenance of the school in addition to the grant from the government of about $64 per head for each pupil". The school closed on the 31st day of March, 1861. Since then, it was kept on the same plans as the public schools in the province of Ontario.[166]

By 1848, there were three hundred and fifty acres of land tamed from the wilderness. The Alderville population totalled two hundred and twenty people – forty-five families living in fifty houses.[167]

From 1850 to 1854, the school was highly regarded by both the Indian Department and the Missionary Society; but from 1855 - 1860, attitudes completely reversed. Was it coincidental that the changes occurred the same year as Father Case died?

In 1855, there was an inspection of both Mount Elgin and Alnwick, and it was recommended that the Alnwick [Alderville] school be closed and the entire population moved to another residential school.

"The Alnwick school...was not satisfactory. The children were not nearly so clean, nor were their dormitories and other apartments kept well ventilated, or in good order, as at Mount Elgin. I was much too pressed for time to hold an examination of the children, but they appeared decidedly less intelligent; and the itch, which was very prevalent, spoke little for the cleanly habits inculcated. The boys had, however, done work about the house neatly and well, and some of the lads who have completed their course are a credit to it... I may add that I purposely visited Alnwick without any warning. This was not the case at Mount Elgin. This circumstance could not, however, have caused the marked difference I saw".[168]

The Alnwick school was still in operation in 1860, but from 1858 to 1860, there were no enrolment figures. A report in 1858 claims that the school did not warrant the expense, and recommended that it be closed and used for other public purposes. The commissioner's report stated that the children had learned "to regard the establishment rather as a prison than a place where they might acquire the means of advancing themselves, and improving their position in the country."[169]

Seven boys graduated from Alnwick and became teachers on reserves but the majority of alumni tended to have aversions to any trade—even the ministry to which they'd been subjected. Missionary reports from 1848 describe a busy scene of farming, but less than ten years later, many of the women had resumed basket-making as a means of supporting themselves.[170]

When the government and the Methodists didn't get the results they sought to achieve, all the blame was laid on the Indians. Thomas Hurlburt, who worked at Alderville from 1851 to 1854, wrote of the insensitivity paid to the Indian people who were equal in God's eyes.[171] Already the school was very much like a child labour camp but the government recommended even harsher administration – that the children should start school when they were younger than the age of ten, and should have *no* contact with other Indians.

The Methodist and government conquest of the Indians didn't stop when their efforts in Upper Canada failed—they went elsewhere, the focus directed to more remote regions, like Hudson's Bay.

Between the 1820s and 30s, the Methodists had approximately fifty active Indian missionaries on the road—not including exhorters or class leaders. But, by 1858, the smaller missions had only occasional preachers, and by 1860 only eight Indian missions were staffed with resident missionaries.

Indian membership in the Methodist Society in eleven years dropped from 1,232 members in 1831, to 772 members in 1842. By the 1850s, the Methodists had lost faith in their Indian missionary leadership.[172]

The death of William Case in 1855 was followed by Peter Jones a year later. New requirements in the Missionary Society

demanded that all Indian missionaries attend Victoria College—
formerly Upper Canada Academy, in Cobourg. The school was
to be a vehicle for "promoting the educational and moral
interests of Upper Canada and of the aboriginal tribes of that
province." The Indians were used as a bargaining chip in a plea
for funds from the government for its construction, yet fewer
than twenty Indian students ever entered the academy's
hallowed halls.[173]   And while the Methodists promoted
temperance, they weren't loathe to accepting funds from those
who benefited from its consumption: in 1832, Dr. John Gilchrist,
a distiller in Keene, laid the cornerstone for the academy.[174]

The Lonely Ones

"Niineta kashkendam nwiigiiwemin", the little girls whimper, clinging to each other. The biggest one strokes the little girls who lean against her. Sarah has felt alone and lonely too; she says nothing, but tears gather in her eyes when she hears them. They cry for their mothers, their grandmothers. They want to see their fathers and brothers and sisters. The little girls call names to the wind but they are a long way from home and no one except the teachers and Black Coats can hear them.

It is September, 1838. Indian Summer. On their own, they would be on the lakes, gathering wild rice; but the lake seems a long distance away, and the days are very different now. Sarah and her people do not know that when they had stopped visiting the rice beds, when the dancing and *mnoomin* ceremonies ended, when the *Ojibway* language was no longer heard, the wild rice had vanished too – and that its demise, coincidental or not, had occurred with the arrival of Christianity.

It is harvest time, but now the crops grow in long rows. And when they aren't bringing in the crops for winter, they are in school. The young women sit with slates in front of them, learning sums. The teacher draws lines and squares on the board to show them where they live. It is called a village and has a main road running through it, with roads cutting off the main one. They are not footpaths. Horses and wagons can travel on them. The men had spent two hundred days building them, and cut one thousand, two hundred and nine logs for their sawmill.

Sarah draws what measures almost three squares – one hundred and fifty acres—on the map of the land where they live, to show her children what has been made ready for buildings or gardens. Two hundred and eight people live in the village now.

The government pays for the houses with the Indians' money—their annuities. The Indians also pay for their sawmill. The preacher's house and barn are built with money from the Black Coats, and the cost of the school is shared by the Black

Coats and the Indians. Twenty-two of the three-room houses built in 1839 by a man from Kingston, are clapboard with brick chimneys and shingled roofs. The houses measure eighteen feet by twenty-six feet with twelve foot posts. Each has four windows on the ground floor, and one upstairs. The remaining fourteen log-houses won't be finished for some time.

Father Case is with them now, and they have a school where Indian children come from other places. They come with the Black Coats; blankets and a few clothes are all they bring. Father Case doesn't want the children to see their mothers and fathers; he says they won't learn anything if they stay with their own kind.[175]

The Lonely Ones hear a voice calling to them from the fields where the hay has been cut and lies flat. The children follow the sound. It is Father Case, singing as he swipes a rake at the grass, gathering it into piles. He beckons to them, and the ones who are not so timid begin to pick up handfuls of the grass and place it on the piles next to him. When they finish, he leads them to a tree near the school.

A rope hangs in a loop from one of the branches. Holding a length of it in each hand, he sits on the loop it makes, then runs backwards as far as the rope will go. When it is taut, he lifts his feet off the ground, and swings back and forth, through the air. The children snicker and wait in a group beside the tree, hoping they'll be given a turn on the swinging rope.

It is 1841. Thirteen Lonely Ones are with them now. When they go to school, there are twenty-five boys in one school with an Indian teacher. The boys spend six hours in school each day, except when seeds must be planted. During the rest of the time, they learn about farming. There are ten in the school for the girls who also go to school six hours every day. When they aren't learning things like geography, they learn needlework or housework.

The children must be out of bed during the winter at five o'clock; and in summer at half past four. In the darkness, the girls herd the cows in from the field to be milked, later, lugging pails back to be separated for cream. Then they make breakfast for their families. After breakfast, each family prays, and then, they meet in a group at the meeting house. Someone will talk about the Bible. Everything is spoken—the singing—everything is in English. The girls churn the cream, then set the cheese and do housework until nine o'clock, when the bell rings for school. Mrs. Case says they have sold more than three thousand pounds of cheese.

Dinner is at noon, then at half past one, they trudge back to school. The needles the girls use to sew with are sharp and shiny; they must wear little metal cups so their fingers don't get speared. They learn housework—how to tuck bedcovers under the ticking, to mop floors. They do this until half past four. They will soon start to spin the wool of sheep and to weave.[176] After supper they have to milk the cows again, and then get cleaned up before a half-hour of prayers at eight. Sarah collapses into slumber each night, weary from the labours of caring for her growing family, but she knows the children—the Lonely Ones— cry themselves to sleep.

One hired man works with the boys now. By summer's end, the boys are like old men, bent and limping, dragging themselves home from the fields. They have cut thirty acres of hay, twenty-five acres of wheat, seven acres of peas and oats. Two hundred bushels of potatoes, eighty bushels of turnips, and fifty bushels of carrots lie in cribs for winter supplies. And when they aren't farming, they cut all the wood for ten stoves and fireplaces to cook on and to keep them warm. Disease has followed them to the Alnwick Mission; it's in the rest of the country that is known as Upper Canada. Measles came in 1846. Typhus, the "lingering sickness from which they died ", was merciless. [177]

In 1852, during a cholera epidemic, Allan Salt was helping the sick and dying, and he became sick too. He appeared to be dead, and the Indians were planning to bury him. His wife asked that they leave her husband another day. They waited. On the third day, when the Indians come to remove the body, Salt does not speak, but gets enough strength to raise himself up off the bed. Then he falls back again. He tells them later that, while he lay sick and dying, he prayed that if his life was spared—from the illness and from being buried alive – that he would devote the rest of his life to the conversion of his people. His wife was so grateful that she, too, gives her life to God's work among the Indian people. He becomes a preacher.

At 2 o'clock on the Monday after New Year's, the doors of the chapel open at Hiawatha, on the north shore of Rice Lake. Long tables covered in white cloths line the hall. The Alderville Indians are guests of their friends. The women have spent hours preparing, and now steaming platters of roasted goose, turkey, ham and venison, stewed beaver and beavers' tails, and wild rice are laid on the tables. Plum pudding finishes the meal, and all but the women push back their chairs and head for the shoreline, where a rink has been shovelled off for skating. The women remain to clear the tables and to bring out tea and baking, to serve when their guests return.

In 1853, twenty-one boys and ten girls—ten to eighteen years old—go to school at the Alderville Mission. The children look after one hundred and five animals. The girls spin wool now, and with the sixty-five pounds of wool spun that year, they knit eighty pairs of stockings, socks and mittens. They make thirteen bed quilts, seventy pairs of trousers and coats for the boys, plus their own clothing. They also wash and iron clothes, milk cows, churn butter and make cheese.[178]

The teachers and missionaries watch everything the children do. The children must never speak Indian or they will be punished. The Black Coats say that the Indian Department wants the students to work even harder. If they work harder they won't need the help of the Great Father. In 1850, thirty-five children come to Alderville from northern schools and are not allowed to see their families until two years later. When they can go home, only ten or eleven return to Alderville.

The men have cleared seventy-six acres of the two hundred-acre farm by 1855. The children are learning to read and write and to do sums, to look at the world on maps and to know the stars by their names. There is only one hour to play each day. Sarah's cousin, Susan Rice, died that spring, of consumption, and by fall, typhus has taken so many little ones the school is closed and the rest of the children go home to live with their families. [179]

Mounds of fresh soil dot the hillside of the cemetery. The men have been busily digging graves to bury their dead. But this day in October, their arms hang at their sides. They have no strength to lift the shovels; the earth they must turn is for the grave of Father Case. He'd fought the diseases that came to the village, but a fall from a horse's back had broken his leg and when he had to remain in bed, bedsores had gouged his body. Fever followed and took him. He died on a Friday and was buried on Sunday. Many Black Coats came from the east and the west.

The Indians knew how Father Case had loved them. They had cried at just the idea of him dying ten years before, when he'd been sick and thought he was going to die. At that time, he'd requested of the people he was with in Montreal, that if he died, his body was to be sent to Alderville and buried with his dear people. But if his body couldn't be sent, that his head, his heart and his hands be buried there: his head that had held the idea of gathering them together and starting a mission; his heart that held his feelings for them, and his hands that had worked for these things.[180] The wish was granted ten years later. His body was in the cemetery, though it pained the Indians to have him departed from them.

Widow Case went north to visit the Indians there and to try to get their children back in school. When the school opened again in 1856, nine Alderville children join thirty Lonely Ones. That year there were sometimes as many as fifty-one students. Some wander away when they go to the fields to work. Others leave in the darkness of night. By late spring, there are only twenty boarders, and by 1857, children stop coming from the north—when they go home for holidays, the parents won't let them return.

Uncle John suffers greatly from the losses of his friends and family. Losing Father Case has been a shocking blow, for he was the connection; he'd been responsible for the changes in their lives, had defended them. Uncle John had lost more than a mortal friend. A year before they came to know Father Case, fifty of Uncle John's people had died. Eleven years after their conversion, they had increased by twenty.

A short year after the death of Father Case, Peter Jones was gone too...then Uncle John's young granddaughter...then his brother on Christmas Day. By 1859, all but one of his children had passed on. His last surviving son and his wife try to comfort him in his sorrow. Uncle John had been a preacher for forty-three years when he retired, and had been a messenger to his people for longer. His eyesight fails him now, though he always attends church. He doesn't know exactly how old he is, but figures to be about eighty—because he fought in the War of 1812 when he was in his late teens.

Uncle John finds comfort in the past; his mind follows memories that sum up his life on earth as if to prepare him for his passing on. He remembers a prophecy that a conjuror told him when the conjuror was not able to work his medicine on people any more. Spirits had told him that two men in black would arrive on an island, and the time and day they would arrive. The prophesy was simple for Uncle John to understand;

he'd seen it come to fruition.

They move Uncle John's bed into the parlour where there would be more room for visitors. Brother Beaver never leaves his side now. People come; they sing and pray with the man who'd been their Head; they were mere bodies, empty vessels without him. When he finally becomes unable to speak, Brother Beaver remains. He recalls for his dying friend the work he'd done, of his accomplishments among his people.

The words give Uncle John energy; he appears soothed, calm, even though he is in pain.[181] He dies in the middle of December, 1875. The church is filled with family, friends, and acquaintances; many have come from far away places to attend the funeral. They carry Uncle John's coffin to the cemetery and bury him next to Father Case. The cemetery is a place that Sarah visits often. Many of her family and friends are there now: her husband, two of their babies, now her uncle, and all but one of his children.

The women now fill their hours making baskets to sell; some will be used to package maple sugar, some will be stacked in nests of varying sizes and sold as one, others will be colourfully decorated with dyed quills. Sarah ties her youngest granddaughter in a sling on her back, and joins the other women to gather berries for dyes and birchbark for making baskets. She offers tobacco, as her mother had, for the gifts each plant gave her. She thanks the spirit of a dead porcupine that gives its quills to her.

Sarah's mother visits her in dreamtime and reminds her of patterns she'd used in her famous quillwork. Her mother speaks to her in Ojibway, calls her *Ishpiniibin*. She tells her about generations to come. Little girls in traditional costumes, young men in mooseskin leggings and colourful feather headdresses like her uncle used to wear, all dancing to the heartbeat of Mother Earth. She tells Sarah that the silence would end, that the Ojibway culture would be strong once again. That her relations, many generations in the future, would dance proudly here, around the village drum.

Afterword

Every story with more than one character has more than one point of view. During the last century and a half, the story of the *Mississaugas* of Grape Island and later of Alderville, has been narrated by both Native and non-Natives. But the story has been largely celebratory and from a Methodist point of view—or influence. While the stories have justly lauded the work of the Native missionaries, they ignore the strong connection these people had with the land, the customs and the beliefs that had made them a strong society prior to European contact.

Only recently has the perspective been challenged, the Native narrative probed by descendants seeking their roots, rediscovering their heritage.

The journey "from darkness to light" was a behavioural modification experiment of the government and church—of trying to change a people—virtually overnight. The Indians had lived tentative lives previous to contact with the white man; they had depended on the hunt and on the fruits of the seasons. In the "light" they were meant to compete—in a new language— with sophisticated European methods, and were supposedly to be treated as equals. But the Indians were called Children; they in turn called government officials Father, and put a childlike trust in their new white parents.

Governmental policies to *deal with them* changed like the seasons. The Indians surrendered thousands of acres of land they had previously traversed freely. The government then doled out plots of land to them, but unlike the white settlers, the Indians were not given deeds to their land. They cleared it, planted and worked the soil, and more often than not, were removed to other places.

By the 1790's, the Indians were already a consumer society- to the point that they needed European blacksmiths to repair their guns.[182] Male self-esteem was low: the male warrior, victorious hunter and trapper was finding it increasingly difficult to provide for his family. Fur traders and settlers plied them with alcohol until they were drunk, then abused and contaminated the women with disease, and cheated the men of money for their furs. Alcohol became the drug that would deaden the pain. And at this low point in their lives, the Black Coat men of the churches arrived to carry out their own clean-up crusade.

All three groups: the government, the Methodists and the Indians—all needed each other at the same time. The Indians were starving dependants; the expense of keeping them weighed heavy on the government that was trying to please the settlers too. The Methodists, campaigning for Christ, sought pagan souls to convert. Their notion of "collecting and civilizing" the Indians in order to teach them Christian ways through learning to read the Scriptures, to write, and to farm was thought to be a step towards their self-sufficiency. Government wanted to establish model communities, and both Grape Island and the Alnwick Mission were fine proposals.[183]

The journey from darkness was a timely one. With the government's expropriation of the Indians' lands and subsequent plans for colonization, settlers—or "Hats" as the Native people called them—sought refuge in Upper Canada, fleeing overpopulation, the effects of war, and famine that were rampant in Europe. With them they brought diseases: cholera, typhus, measles and scarlet fever. The Native people were unable to combat these new diseases and whole camps quickly succumbed to the viruses.[184] Until that time, diseases common among the Indian population had been consumption, fever, pleurisy and other respiratory ailments from living in a severe climate. Intestinal parasites and dysentery were common ailments caused from the meat they sometimes ate raw. Only those with the strongest constitutions survived in the extreme conditions and more than half the children born then died before adolescence.[185]

When the Indians became Christians, and sought to have their children educated—and have better lives—they were prohibited from speaking their language. Mothers and fathers, grandmothers and grandfathers spoke among themselves: low tones in *Ojibway*, but only in private. They stopped immediately a child came in the room.

Until the arrival of the white man, there had been no written language; petroglyphs—like the Teaching Rocks at Stoney Lake and Lake Superior, like the birch bark scrolls—were the sacred and respected documents of the day.[186] The images etched into the rocks were records of dreams, of visions received during times of fasting. Their authors wanted to communicate this knowledge. The *Ojibway* language was founded in nature; it is utilitarian, descriptive—but only of a vocabulary relevant to their life.[187] Even today, *Ojibway* is a constantly evolving language that has to develop a vocabulary to keep apace with technology and the computerized world. Before the arrival of the Hats, words like cede, surrender, sovereignty, deed, and title had no relevance in their lives.

Initially, pieces of paper were less important than verbal communication because the native people couldn't read. Their signatures were their totem symbols. To other parts of the world where the alphabet had been in use for centuries, levels of written communication ranged from succinct to ambiguous, to downright fraudulent. In those parts of the world there was little respect for the word, and talk was even cheaper. But the bureaucrats knew the value of signatures—even if they were totemic symbols.

What was more important to the Native people at that time was the interpretation—especially from one of their own people. That their Great White Father across the Salt Water had rewarded his Children for their assistance in defending the colonies was something the Chiefs and Principal men could not dispute [that they were called Children was probably not even considered]. Before a document was signed, what the Chiefs and Principal men heard before they signed their totems was the *essence* of what was written on the document. They signed because what they heard through their interpreter sounded good to them.

Oratory was a major selling point to the Native people, and in this area the Methodist exhorters and evangelists were the most charismatic of the period. In comparison, the Anglican Church appealed to a more cerebral, ordered worshipper, and the Roman Catholic Church to those who sought ritual, pomp and ceremony. When the Methodist Movement entered Upper Canada it evolved to meet the needs of the sparsely settled area, and to appeal to the Native population. The itinerant preacher aligned with the nomadic Indians' sensibilities.

The Methodists encountered several strong Native men whom they recruited to become missionaries: the energized exhorters of the Methodist Movement among the aboriginal people and the reason for its success during pre-Confederation.

The Native heroes of the story: Peter Jones, John Sunday,

Allan Salt and others are to be revered for their undying commitment, for the trials and the hardships they endured. Other unsung heroes are their brothers who died after only a few years of itinerancy [John Moses, John Paul, et. al.]. They crossed the country converting their aboriginal brothers from paganism to Christianity. Indian missionaries were economical for the church: they could live off the bounty of the land and knew how to deal with the severity of the climate.

While their children were punished for speaking *Ojibway*—a language that *was* their culture, the Methodists had their Native exhorters—these living triumphs of Christianity—don traditional costumes, complete with tomahawks and scalping knives—to entertain prospective benefactors in the United States and England. While they renounced the use of alcohol in the Methodist Society, they enjoyed the benefits of profits gained by those in the business of selling liquor—donations were graciously accepted.

The popularity of Methodism among the Native people died with its heroes—its role models. What was once undying enthusiasm for the religion atrophied to out-and-out aversion. The side-effect of this forced resocialization process by the Methodists was trauma for the Indian population. This trauma manifested as social amnesia—a culture shock—that has reverberated for several generations.

Resocialization requires more than changing clothes, more than adopting daily habits and learning a new language. The short-term effects were disrespect for the chiefs, for farming and for anything they'd been subjected to in the mission schools. The old frame church that was Alderville's raison d'etre in the formative years of Upper Canada now serves only a fraction of the population.

The move to Alnwick Township was ironic in many ways for the *Mississaugas*. Alderville is only a short distance from Rice Lake—a body of water that had been abundant with wild rice for 9,000 years—dwindling at the beginning of the Christian era. The waters were sacred; it had been a place where tribes brought their elders to bathe in the healing waters. The Alnwick settlement had no access to the water, and the *Mississaugas* were prohibited from fishing on it. Yet while Methodist and government policies dictated that the Indians were to quit hunting and fishing, throughout the period of Grape Island and of early Alderville, the fiscal reality was that fishing and hunting were the only two means of supplementing what would otherwise have been a meagre vegetarian diet.

One member of Alderville First Nation recollects the words of an elder who said that the old ways: culture, language, beliefs and customs, the drum,—would all disappear with the wild rice ... and wouldn't return until it did. He reports that the rice seedlings that were planted a few years ago around the lake have taken. The drum has returned, and with it, ceremonies and celebrations.

Ten years ago, *Ojibway* became a subject in Roseneath Centennial School. Now it continues into secondary school, and parents attend language classes on the reserve. They are taught that language *is* culture, rich and full of tradition, and have come to realize that there is a growing respect for traditional Native culture.

Endnotes

1. See Allan Salt, Indian Methodist Missionary, 1888. Allan Salt, a Mississauga boy adopted by Father William Case, became a teacher and missionary among his people. In 1888 he wrote: "The Indian way of pronouncing the word (mississaga) is *minzezagee* (plural *minzezageeg*) and signified, in the plural, persons who inhabit the country where there are many mouths of the rivers, as the Trent, Moira, Shannon, Napanee, Kingston River and Ganonoque.

2. Footwear or moccasins. an indicates plural (makizin-singular)

3. See COBOURG STAR

4. Berry Moon: July

5. See Peter Jones' HISTORY OF THE OJEBWAY INDIANS, pp.100-101

6. See HISTORY OF THE OJIBWA OF THE CURVE LAKE RESERVE AND SURROUNDING AREA; Vol. II, p.33, for Short Tom Taylor's description.

7. See Basil Johnson's OJIBWAY CEREMONIES, pp.13-15 See also Curve Lake, Vol.II

8. See Christopher Vecsey's TRADITIONAL OJIBWA RELIGION AND ITS HISTORICAL CHANGES, p.111.

9. Ibid.

10. See HISTORY OF THE OJIBWA OF THE CURVE LAKE RESERVE AND SURROUNDING AREA, Vol.II, p.91. See also Ruth Landes' OJIBWA WOMAN, p.2.

11. See Peter Jones' HISTORY OF THE OJEBWAY INDIANS, p. 153: medicinal plants. See also THE JOURNAL OF AMERICAN FOLK-LORE, vol. I, p. 156.

12. See Vecsey's TRADITIONAL OJIBWA RELIGION AND ITS HISTORICAL CHANGES, p.61.

13. See Allan Salt's Journals; Notebook 11: 1872-1901; also William Canniff's SETTLEMENT OF UPPER CANADA, p.30. See also CURVE LAKE: while Jones says Sunday is of the REINDEER, another says MINK.

14. Allan Salt, Indian Methodist Missionary, 1888. See also "THE COMING OF THE MISSISSAGAS", address by Robert Paudash to Peterborough Historical Society, vol.6 (1905) Ontario Historical Society.

15. Ojibway Months (Giisook) of the Year: Mnidoo Giizis: Spirit Moon:

January; Mkwa Giizis: Bear Moon: February; Naabdin Giizis: Snowcrust Moon: March; Boopoogame Giizis: Broken Snowshoe Moon: April; Nmebine Giizis: Sucker Moon: May; Waabgonii Giizis: Blooming Moon: June; Miin Giizis: Berry Moon: July; Mnoomnii Giizis: Grain Moon: August; Waabab'gaa Giizis: Autumn Moon: September; Bnaakwii Giizis: Falling Leaves Moon: October; Baashkaakoodin Giizis: Freezing Moon: November; Mnidoo Giisoonhs: Little Spirit Moon: December—Melody Crowe, Ojibway Instructor. See also Peter Jones' THE HISTORY OF THE OJEBWAY INDIANS, p.135-136.

16.   See George Copway's THE TRADITIONAL HISTORY AND CHARACTERISTIC SKETCHES OF THE OJIBWAY NATION.

17.   See HISTORY OF THE OJIBWA OF THE CURVE LAKE RESERVE AND SURROUNDING AREA. Vol. II p.72. See also Allan Salt's Notebook: 1872-1901

18.   See Vecsey, p.83

19.   Makizin singular. **an** denotes plural.

20.   See Ruth Landes' OJIBWA WOMAN, p.128

21.   Jones, Peter; HISTORY OF THE OJEBWAY INDIANS. "Treatment of the Women by the Men" p.60.

21a   Jones' HISTORY OF THE OJEBWAY INDIANS, p. 139

22.   See Vecsey; p.15

23.   See Brookings' Obituary in Methodist Church Minutes of Third Toronto Conference 1876 "Who Have Died? John Sunday".

24.   See Captain F. Moore's INDIAN PLACE NAMES

25.   See Ruth Landes' OJIBWA WOMAN

26.   Fried bread; bannock.

27.   See CURVE LAKE, Vol. II; p.96

28.   See OJIBWA WOMAN, p.11.

29.   See Vecsey, p.64.

30.   See Jones' HISTORY OF THE OJEBWAY INDIANS p.143

31.   See Ruth Landes' OJIBWA WOMAN, p.7

32.   Ibid. pp.124-5

33.   See JOURNAL OF AMERICAN FOLK-LORE, Vol. II, 1889. "Tales of the Mississaguas." pp. 144-5.

34.   See CURVE LAKE; Vol.II, p.96.

35.   See OJIBWA WOMAN. p.5.

35a   Jones' HISTORY OF THE OJEBWAY PEOPLE, pp. 98-101)

36.   Ibid. pp.135-6.

37.   "Last Stand In the Wild Rice Country", HARROWSMITH, #19, Vol.III:7; May 1979.

38.   See JOURNAL OF AMERICAL FOLKLORE Vol.1; "Notes on the Mississaga Indians".

39. See CURVE LAKE Vol.II, pp. 63-64.
40. See OJIBWA WOMAN, p. 15.
41. See CURVE LAKE Vol. II, p.25.
42. See HISTORY OF THE OJEBWAY INDIANS, p.73.
43. Ibid. pp.135.
44. See Allan Salt's Journals; Notebook #11: 1872-1901.
45. See Jones' HISTORY OF THE OJEBWAY INDIANS. p.55: A legend related by Chief Netahgawinene, of Cold Water.
46. See OJIBWA WOMAN, p. 31.
47. See CURVE LAKE, Vol. II, p.25.
48. OJIBWA WOMAN; pp.214-5
49. Anishnaabeg is the name given to the people of the Great Lakes region. Literally translated, the combination of words meaning "without cause" or "spontaneous" and "human body". Combined: "spontaneous man." – CURVE LAKE, Vol.1.p.1. See also THE MISHOMIS BOOK, p.3.
50. See Peter Jones' LIFE AND JOURNALS OF KAH-KE-WA-QUO-NA-BY, p.58.
51. See Morris', INDIANS OF ONTARIO
52. See Berton's INVASION OF CANADA p.21-26. See also Maclean's HIDDEN AGENDA. Ch.3.
53. See French's PARSONS AND POLITICS pp. 47-54.
54. See Taylor's thesis p.77
55. INDIAN WOMEN AND THE LAW: CITIZENS MINUS; p.9
56. Berton, Pierre; INVASION OF CANADA pp.40-41
57. See Morris' INDIANS OF ONTARIO.
58. Taylor's thesis, pp.59-60
59. French, Goldwyn; PARSONS AND POLITICS. pp.40-44
60. French's essay in HISTORICAL ESSAYS ON UPPER CANADA etc.p.540
61. French; PARSONS p.108
62. Methodist Episcopal Church Reports for 1825, p. 7
63. See Sissons' EGERTON RYERSON: HIS LIFE AND LETTERS, Vol. I, p. 39
64. See Canniff's SETTLEMENT OF UPPER CANADA,pp.295-6
65. From a telephone interview with Rev. Arthur Kewley.
66. See Kewley's thesis: "Mass Evangelism in Upper Canada Before 1830" See also Moodie's LIFE IN THE CLEARINGS. pp.140-141.
67. See Sissons p.25.
68. See Jones' HISTORY OF THE OJEBWAY INDIANS pp. 227-228.
69. Goldwyn French writing of the Conference's decision of appointing Case as General Superintendent. Dictionary of Canadian Biography p.133 See also "A CIRCUIT RIDER ON THE RIVER

THAMES"
70. Dictionary of Canadian Biography says 18; editors of Jones' HISTORY OF THE OJEBWAY INDIANS say he was 16.
71. Jones' HISTORY OF THE OJEBWAY INDIANS.p.5-9.
72. Maclean's HIDDEN AGENDA. p.36
73. Jones' HISTORY OF THE OJEBWAY INDIANS, p.4
74. DICTIONARY OF CANADIAN BIOGRAPHY.
75. MacLean's HIDDEN AGENDA. pp.80-81
76. See Carroll's CASE AND HIS COTEMPORARIES[sic]; Vol. III, p.72
77. Taylor's thesis, 40-50 pp.
78. Jones' JOURNALS
79. Rev. Brooking in Missionary Notices of the Methodist Church of Canada; 3rd series #6 March 1876
80. See Smith's SACRED FEATHERS p.92. See also HISTORY OF OJEBWAY INDIANS "Dress" pp. 75-77
81. Vecsy, pp.4,5
82. See Maclean's VANGUARDS OF CANADA. p.21
83. See Graham's MEDICINE MAN TO MISSIONARY p.10
84. 2nd Annual Report of the Canada Conference Missionary Society Auxiliary to the Missionary Society. St. Catherines,1826. See August 15,1826 Belleville Missionary Society report to 2nd Annual Report of the Canada Conference, p.8. Also Jones' LIFE AND JOURNALS OF KAKEWAQUONABY, p.53.
85. See Playter's HISTORY OF METHODISM, p.277.
86. See Maclean's VANGUARDS OF CANADA: ch.2. " Shawundais: The Orator"
87. See MISSIONARY NOTICES OF THE METHODIST CHURCH OF CANADA, 3rd series, #6,March 1876-"Death of The Rev. John Sunday" from Rev. Robert Brooking, dated Alderville, December 30,1875.
88. Methodist Church Minutes of 1876 Conference-3rd Toronto Conf.p12. Who Have Died? John Sunday.
89. "the heavens"
90. See Playter's HISTORY OF METHODISM. p.276
91. See Smith's SACRED FEATHERS p.93
92. Shawundais was originally from New York State, where another dialect would be spoken. The southern Ontario dialect: "Gzhe-Mnidoo zhawenmishin"—Melody Crowe.
93. Playter, p.278
94. Carroll, CASE AND HIS COTEMPORARIES [sic] Vol. III, p. 114; Vol. IV. p.269
95. Kewley's thesis
96. Playter's HISTORY OF METHODISM. p.280.

97. HISTORY OF THE OJIBWA OF THE CURVE LAKE RESERVE AND SURROUNDING AREA, Vol.I, p.62.

98. See Maclean's HIDDEN AGENDA, pp.29-30. See also CHRISTIAN GUARDIAN, 17 July 1833.Methodist Missionary Society (Canada) Annual Report, 1827

99. See French's essay in HISTORICAL ESSAYS ON UPPER CANADA. p.355

100. Cornish' s CYCLOPEDIA OF METHODISM IN CANADA

101. See Playter's HISTORY OF METHODISM IN CANADA, p.226

102. See Boehme's THE MISSION ON GRAPE ISLAND pp.15,16

103. See P.A.C.: R.G.1,E.3.Vol.33,p.93. See also P.A.C.: R.G.1, G.3.,Vol.33, pp.93,94.

104 GUARDIAN, October 15,1834,p.194

105 Ibid.

106. Jones' JOURNALS pp. 68-69.

107. Playter's HISTORY OF METHODISM IN CANADA, p.279

108. Jones' JOURNALS

109. See Ontario Historical Society, Vol.27, pp. 540-542.

110. 2nd Annual Report of the Canada Conference

111. See Canniff's SETTLEMENT OF UPPER CANADA. p.326

112. Jones' JOURNALS. Chapter 3.

113. Playter's HISTORY OF METHODISM. p.280.

114. See Carroll's CASE & COTEMPORARIES. Vol.III,p.452

115. See Guillet's EARLY LIFE IN UPPER CANADA. 1933. p.298

116. See Playter's HISTORY OF METHODISM. p.281

117. See Waldron's A SKETCH OF THE LIFE, TRAVELS, AND LABOURS OF SOLOMON WALDRON, WESLEYAN METHODIST PREACHER, BY THE AUTHOR. p.25

118. 3rd Report of the Missionary Society 1827

119. Waldron's A SKETCH OF THE LIFE, TRAVELS AND LABOURS OF SOLOMON WALDRON, WESLEYAN METHODIST PREACHER, BY THE AUTHOR.

120. Francis Hall's report on his visit to Grape Island, 24-26 August, 1828. Class No.1- John Paul, leader; Gilbert Snake, Elizabeth Snake, Phoebe Moses, Jane Moses, Laura Shipegraw, Ann Johnson, Rebecca Otter, Peggy Otter, Jacob Snowstorm, Elizabeth Skunk, Nancy Culberson, Peter Thomas, and Jacob Shipyou.
     Class No.2- William Beaver, leader; John Johnson, Margaret Beaver, Diana Paul, Betsey Abrahams, Jane Nebenner, Mary Handkerchief, Peggy Thomas, Esther Crow, Hannah Nebenner, William Scott, Lois Thomas, Nancy Shipegraw, Mary Kameksan, Polly Bird, Jacob Sunday.
     Class No.3- Joseph Skunk,leader; John Skunk, Catherine Beaver,

Polly Culberson, George Crow, David Crow, John Salt, Isaac Skunk, Betsey Otter, Mysneir, Mary Crowbreach, James Bird, Elizabeth Snowstorm and Elizabeth Doctor.

Class No.4- James Crawford, leader; Peter Shipegraw, Margaret Shipegraw, Elizabeth Jacob, Paul Yowesonk, Patta Snake, Jane Culberson, Polly Snake, Jenny Crow, Peggy Michael, Susan Paul, Jenny Wilkins, Mary Sunday, senior, and Mary Sunday, junior.

Class No.5- John Simpson, leader; James Buck, John Snake, John Pigeon, Hannah Snake, Rachel Howard, Mary Ann Snake, Sally Buck, Catharine Crow, Anna Jacob, Mary Shipegraw, Jane Nelson, and Mary Handkerchief.

Class No.6- John Sunday, leader; James Jack, Nelson Snake, William Cunnego [Comego?], Henry Snake, James Indian, Mary Indian, Charles Jacob, Robert Wilkins, Mary Crawford, Rachel Salt, Tobias Frazer, Peter Crow and Samuel Skunk

121. Maclean's VANGUARDS OF CANADA. p.23. See also Boehme, p.14.

122. See 21 Sept.1831 in Waldron's A SKETCH.

123. See Jones'JOURNALS. p.157

124. Ibid. pp.177, 262.

125. Ibid. p.184

126. See Carroll's CASE & HIS COTEMPORARIES[sic]. Vol.3, p.227.

127. Boehme, p.18

128. Methodist Episcopal Church Reports of the period ending Sept.1, 1829.

129. Carroll's CASE & HIS CO. Vol.III, p.281

130. CHRISTIAN GUARDIAN. Oct.30,1830 Vol.1, #50, p.394-402.

131. Jones' JOURNALS. p.279

132. Jones' HISTORY OF THE OJEBWAY INDIANS. p.175

133. CHRISTIAN GUARDIAN, Vol.II, #.2, p.6

134. 1831: Minutes of the Annual Conferences 1824-1845

135. CHRISTIAN GUARDIAN, Jan.16,1858, p.58

136. P.A.C.: R.G.1, E3, Vol.33, pp.92,92a.

137. Graham's MEDICINE MAN TO MISSIONARY. p.53

138. CHRISTIAN GUARDIAN, Vol. II, #50. Thomas Frazier and Joseph Skunk go with Sunday.

139. 6th Annual Report, p.30

140. Carroll's CASE & HIS CO., Vol.III, pp.289, 325,402.

141. Jones' JOURNALS. p.40

142. CHRISTIAN GUARDIAN, 2 October 1833, p.186. See also THE CHILDREN'S FRIEND, Vol 14, #157; January 1837

143. See CHRISTIAN GUARDIAN; Vol. IV, #46, pp.182-183

144. See Maclean's VANGUARDS OF CANADA. p.23.

3.

Endnotes 85

145. See Boehme's MISSION ON GRAPE ISLAND. p.26
146. See Smith's SACRED FEATHERS, p. 232
147. Indian Agent Thackeray reporting on Thomas Marsden.
148. See Strickland's 27 YEARS IN CANADA WEST or THE EXPERIENCE OF AN EARLY SETTLER.
149. Sully Road runs south to Harwood, off Northumberland County Road #9.
150 See Carroll's CASE AND HIS CO., Vol. IV, p.132.
151 See James Evan's Diary 1838.
152. See Smith's SACRED FEATHERS. p.164.
153. See Maclean's VANGUARDS OF CANADA. pp.24-25.
154. Jones' HISTORY OF THE OJEBWAY INDIANS, p.258-261.
155. See History of Women's Institute
156. CHRISTIAN GUARDIAN, 19 September,1838. p. 182
157. Guillet's EARLY LIFE IN UPPER CANADA. pp.300-301
158. Methodist Missionary Society's Records (Wesleyan Methodist, England) Minutes. Upper Canada, 1837-1847.
159. Graham's MEDICINE MAN TO MISSIONARY. p.26
159a Maclean, HIDDEN AGENDA. pp. 17,18
160. Ibid.
161. See CHRISTIAN GUARDIAN, 12 Dec.1849.
162. See Graham's MEDICINE MAN TO MISSIONARY. p. 27
163. Maclean's HIDDEN AGENDA. p.98
164. Ibid.
165. Carroll's CASE & CO. Vol.IV, p.208
166. Historical Society; THE SENTINAL STAR (Cobourg) May 9,1902
167. Rev. Enoch Wood, in "Christmas Among the Indians"
168. Viscount Bury to Edmund_Head, 5 December, 1855; Indian Department, 1856.
169. Maclean's HIDDEN AGENDA p.97
170. Methodist Society Report 1848: XXII; 1857: XXIX.
171. Missionary Society Reports 1859: XVII.
172. See Maclean's HIDDEN AGENDA.
173. Ibid.
174. Sissons, p.296
175. Carroll's CASE & CO.Vol.IV,p.265
176. Graham's MEDICINE MAN TO MISSIONARY. p.77
177. Missionary Society Reports for 1848:xxiv;1851,1852xvi,1856 xxii.
178. Missionary Society Reports for 1851
179. Missionary Society Reports 1852: XVI, See also HIDDEN AGENDA
180. Carroll, CASE & HIS COTEMPORARIES [sic]; Vol.IV, p.487

181. Brooking's "DEATH OF THE REV. JOHN SUNDAY"
182. See Donald Smith's essay "The Dispossession of the Mississauga Indians". See Anna Jameson's WINTER STUDIES AND SUMMER RAMBLES, and Canniff's description of the Mississaguas in SETTLEMENT OF UPPER CANADA.
183. See Graham's MEDICINE MAN TO MISSIONARY, pp.23,24
184. See Journal of American Folklore Vol 1, p.156.
185. See Jones' HISTORY OF THE OJEBWAY INDIANS. pp. 141-142.
186. See video, Teaching Rocks.
187. See "Mother Tongue", CANADIAN WOMEN'S STUDIES, Vol.10,# 2,3, 1989, pp. 69,70

Bibliography

Benton-Banai, THE MISHOMIS BOOK: The Voice of the Ojibway; St. Paul Minn.: Red School House, 1988.

Berton, Pierre, THE INVASION OF CANADA, 1812-1813; Toronto: McClelland & Stewart, 1980.

Boehme, Richard; THE MISSION ON GRAPE ISLAND; Bloomfield: 7th Town Historical Society,1966.

Canniff, William; SETTLEMENT OF UPPER CANADA; Belleville: Mika Silk Screening Ltd., 1971 (reprint).

Carroll, John; CASE & HIS COTEMPORARIES [sic], Volumes III, IV; Toronto: Methodist Bookroom, 1871.

Copway, George; INDIAN LIFE AND INDIAN HISTORY; Boston: Colby, 1858.

_____, THE TRADITIONAL HISTORY AND CHARACTERISTIC SKETCHES OF THE OJIBWAY NATION; Boston: B.B. Mussey, 1986.

Cornish, George H., CYCLOPEDIA OF METHODISM IN CANADA; Toronto: Methodist Book Room and Publishing House,1903.

French, Goldwin, PARSONS AND POLITICS: The Role of the Wesleyan Methodists in Upper Canada and the Maritimes from 1780 to 1855. Toronto: Ryerson Press, 1962.

_____, "Egerton Ryerson and the Methodist Model for Upper Canada", HISTORICAL ESSAYS ON UPPER CANADA: NEW PERSPECTIVES. Ottawa: Carleton University Press Inc., 1989.

Graham, Elizabeth, MEDICINE MAN TO MISSIONARY: Missionaries as Agents of Change among the Indians of Southern Ontario, 1784-1867. Toronto: Peter Martin Associates, 1975.

Guillet, Edwin,C. EARLY LIFE IN UPPER CANADA. (1933), Toronto: reprint University of Toronto Press, 1963,1967.

Halpenny, Frances G., ed., DICTIONARY OF CANADIAN BIOGRAPHY, Vol.III 1851-1860. Toronto: University of Toronto Press, 1985.

Jameson, Anna; WINTER STUDIES AND SUMMER RAMBLES IN CANADA. (1837) Toronto: McClelland and Stewart, reprinted 1923.

Jamieson, Kathleen; INDIAN WOMEN AND THE LAW IN CANADA: CITIZENS MINUS, Advisory Council on the Status of Women: Indian Rights for Indian Women; Ottawa: Minister of Supply and Services. 1978.

Johnson, Basil; INDIAN SCHOOL DAYS. Toronto: Key Porter Books, 1988.

_____, OJIBWAY CEREMONIES.Toronto: McClelland and Stewart, 1982.

Johnson, J.K. and Bruce G. Wilson; HISTORICAL ESSAYS ON UPPER CANADA: NEW PERSPECTIVES. Ottawa: Carleton University Press Inc., 1989.

Jones, Peter; HISTORY OF THE OJEBWAY INDIANS. London: A.W.Bennett,1861.

Landes, Ruth; OJIBWA WOMAN. New York: AMS Press. 1938. reprint 1969

Maclean, John; VANGUARDS OF CANADA. Toronto: The Missionary Society of the Methodist Church,1918.

Moir, John S. Ed., WESTERN ONTARIO HISTORICAL NUGGETS #25, "A Circuit Rider on the River Thames"—the diary of William Case, 20 June-26 August, 1809. London: Lawson Memorial Library, University of Western Ontario, 1958.

Moodie, Susanna; LIFE IN THE CLEARINGS VERSUS THE BUSH.(1853) Toronto: McClelland and Stewart: New Canadian Library reprint 1989.

_____, ROUGHING IT IN THE BUSH. (1852) London: Virago Press. reprint 1986

Moore, Captain F., INDIAN PLACE NAMES; Toronto: Macmillan, 1930.

Morris, J.L., C.E.,D.E., INDIANS OF ONTARIO. Toronto: Dept. of Lands and Forests, 1943. reprinted 1964.

Newell, W.W., ed., THE JOURNAL OF AMERICAN FOLK-LORE, Vol.I, "Notes on the History, Customs and Beliefs of the Mississauga". New York: Kraus Reprint Corporation, 1963.

_____, THE JOURNAL OF AMERICAN FOLK-LORE, Vol.II , "Tales of the Mississaugas" (1889). New York: Kraus Reprint Corporation, 1963.

Playter, Geo. Frederick; THE HISTORY OF METHODISM IN CANADA. Toronto: Anson Green, 1862.

Roseneath Women's Institute; HISTORY OF THE WOMEN'S INSTITUTE: TWEEDSMUIR HISTORY. Bowmanville: Mothersill Printing, Inc. 1981.

Sissons, EGERTON RYERSON: HIS LIFE AND LETTERS-Vol.1.Toronto: Clarke Irwin & Company,1937.

Smith, Donald; SACRED FEATHERS: The Reverend Peter Jones (Kahkewaquonaby) and the Mississauga Indians. Toronto: University of Toronto Press, 1987.

_____, "The Dispossession of the Mississauga Indians: a Missing Chapter in the Early History of Upper Canada", HISTORICAL ESSAYS ON UPPER CANADA: NEW PERSPECTIVES. Ottawa: Carleton University Press Inc., 1989.

Stevens, Abel; THE LIFE AND TIMES OF NATHAN BANGS. New York: Carlton&Porter,1863.

Strickland, Samuel. 27 YEARS IN CANADA WEST, or THE EXPERIENCE OF AN EARLY SETTLER (1853). Edmonton: Hurtig, reprint 1970.

Traill, Catharine Parr (Rupert Scheider, reprint ed.,.) CANADIAN

CRUSOES: A Tale of the Rice Lake Plains. Ottawa: Carleton University Press,1986.

Vecsey, Christopher; TRADITIONAL OJIBWA RELIGION AND ITS HISTORICAL CHANGES. Philadelphia: American Philosophical Society, 1983.

Waldron, Solomon. A SKETCH OF THE LIFE, TRAVELS AND LABOURS OF SOLOMON WALDRON, WESLEYAN METHODIST PREACHER, BY THE AUTHOR. Toronto: U.C. Archives, ca.1849.

Whetung- Derrick, Mae, ed., HISTORY OF THE OJIBWA OF THE CURVE LAKE RESERVE AND SURROUNDING AREA; 3 vols. Curve Lake: (photocopied) 1976.

JOURNALS

James Evans Diary: 1838. File 6; Toronto: E. J .Pratt Library.

Jones, Peter; LIFE AND JOURNALS OF KAHHEWWAQUONABY; Toronto: Anson Green, 1860.

Reverend Allan Salt Journals. Microfilm c15709. Ottawa: National Archives of Canada.

Reverend Allan Salt: Methodist Missionary 1888. Ottawa: National Archives of Canada

Reverend Allan Salt Notebook 11: 1872-1901. Ottawa: National Archives of Canada.

NATIONAL ARCHIVES OF CANADA

P.A.C. RG 10, E3, Vol. 33, p. 93.
P.A.C. RG 10, G3, Vol. 33, pp. 93, 94.
P.A.C. RG 10, E3, Vol. 33, pp. 92,92a.

UNITED CHURCH ARCHIVES

Belleville Missionary Society Report to the 2nd Annual report of the Canada Conference.

CHRISTIAN GUARDIAN, articles from: Oct.30, 1830 Vol.1, #50; July 17,1833; Oct.2,1833; Sept.19,1838; Dec.12, 1849; Vol.II,#2; Jan.16, 1858; Vol. II-#50;

Methodist Church Minutes: 1876- Toronto Conference.

Methodist Episcopal Church Reports for 1825; Sept.1, 1829.

Methodist Missionary Society (Canada) Annual Report: 1827.

Methodist Missionary Society's Records (Wesleyan Methodist, England) Minutes. Upper Canada, 1837-1847. Microfilm D.6.4.#60

Missionary Notices of the Methodist Church of Canada; 3rd series #6 March 1876

Missionary Society Reports: 1848 xxii; 1857 xxix; 1859 xvii, xxix;

Reynolds, Rev.Arthur G., ed., "Christmas Among The Indians", THE BULLETIN. Toronto: The Committee on Archives, The United Church of Canada, No.16, 1963.

Second Annual Report of the Canada Conference Missionary Society Auxiliary to the Missionary Society of the Methodist Episcopal Church, St. Catharines, 1826.

"A Visit to the Mohawk and Missisaqui [sic] Indians", THE CHILDREN'S FRIEND, #157; Vol.14, Jan.1837. London: British Museum,1837.

PERIODICALS

Avery, Kathi and Thomas Pawlick, "The Last Stand", HARROWSMITH #19, Vol. III:7, Camden East: Camden House Publishing Ltd, 1979.

Burnham, J. Hampden; "The Coming of the Mississaugas". Ontario Historical Society, 1966.

Fedorick, Joy Asham, "Mother Tongue: Aboriginal Cultures and Languages", CANADIAN WOMAN STUDIES. Vol.10, #s 2,3, Downsview: CWS, York University, 1989.

Peterborough Historical Society; Vol.6 (1905) "The Coming of the Mississaugas", address by Robert Paudash.

THESES

Kewley, Arthur; MASS EVANGELISM IN UPPER CANADA BEFORE 1838, D.OF T. Thesis. Toronto: United Church Archives, 1960.

Maclean, Hope; HIDDEN AGENDA: Methodist Attitudes to the Ojibwa and the Development of Indian Schooling in Upper Canada—1821-1860; University of Toronto MA Thesis, 1978.

Smith, Donald B. "The Mississauga, Peter Jones, and the White Man: the Algonkians' Adjustment to the Europeans on the North Shore of Lake Ontario to 1860." Ph.D. thesis, University of Toronto, 1975.

Taylor, Gordon Garfield, "The Mississauga Indians of Eastern Ontario, 1634 – 1881". Kingston: Queen's University, MA Thesis, 1981.

Whyte, Terence T., "Grape Island: Methodist Missionary Station". B OF D thesis, Emmanuel College, University of Toronto, 1965.

NEWSPAPERS

"Historical Society: The Arrival of the Grape Islanders at Rice Lake",
  Cobourg: THE SENTINEL STAR, May 9, 1902.
"Indian Artifacts on Sugar Island", COBOURG STAR, May 29,1973.
"Report to the Chief: Students Dig into their own past at Indian Site",
  COBOURG STAR. May 22, 1974

VIDEO

THE TEACHING ROCKS. Walton, Lloyd, dir. Woodview: Friends of the
  Teaching Rocks.